.......The Digital Delay Handbook.

Amsco Publications.
New York/London/Sydney

Cover design by Pearce Marchbank
Interior design and schematic drawings
by The Bookmakers, Inc.

Order No. AM 38985
International Standard Book Number: 0.8256.2414.2

Exclusive Distributors
Music Sales Corporation
24 East 22nd Street, New York, NY 10010 USA
Music Sales Limited
78 Newman Street, London W1P 3LA England
Music Sales Pty. Limited
27 Clarendon Street, Artarmon, Sydney NSW 2064 Australia

Printed in the United States of America by
Hamilton Printing Company

Contents

Acknowledgment

Thanks to Richard DeFreitas (president of DeltaLab Research) who once said to me, "What this world needs is a digital delay handbook," and thereupon loaned me enough equipment to write it. His encouragement of this project has been most appreciated, especially with respect to multiple delay line applications.

How to Use This Handbook

~~~~~~

Even if you are a digital delay line (DDL) expert, read Chapter 1 carefully since it defines the terms used in the rest of the book. Note that this book assumes that you are familiar with common effects (noise gates, equalizers, reverb) as well as with the terms used with effects (input, output, level). If you need to brush up on this basic knowledge, refer to my previous book, *Guitar Gadgets*.

Chapters 2 through 9 present the various applications; each application follows a standard format. If any additional feature (or equipment) is needed, it is listed just below the application's title and indicated by a +. The text then gives some background on what the application is intended to do, explains how to hook up the equipment, and suggests initial control settings.

Because of variations between different models and brands of delay lines, any suggested control settings are *approximations*. While they should help get you started, it will take some additional tweaking (as described in the final part of each application) to get the sound "just right."

When you find an effect you like, write down the control and switch settings, as well as any notes, for later reference. I suggest making several dozen photocopies of the front panel layout for this purpose.

Digital delay lines are far more versatile than many people realize. Have fun with these applications, and remember—experiment! If you come up with any other interesting applications, write me c/o Music Sales and perhaps I can include them in future editions.

Chapter 1

Understanding Digital Delay Line Controls

〜〜〜〜〜〜〜〜〜〜〜〜〜〜〜〜〜〜〜〜〜

All digital delay lines, regardless of model or manufacturer, have many common functions and controls and can therefore produce many of the same effects. The first part of this chapter describes the functions and controls found on virtually all delay lines; most of the applications in this handbook will work with any delay line that includes these basic features.

The second part of the chapter covers more specialized features, which are available on some delay lines and are required for some of the more unusual applications.

BASIC DELAY LINE FEATURES

Although delay lines have many common features, different manufacturers call them by different names and sometimes have different ways of implementing certain functions. We will note several of these differences when discussing the various controls.

Follow along with your delay line's owner's manual while you read this chapter, and correlate the control names for your device to the control names described below. If you are interested in how these controls relate to the delay line circuitry, refer to **Figure 1-1**, a generalized delay line block diagram.

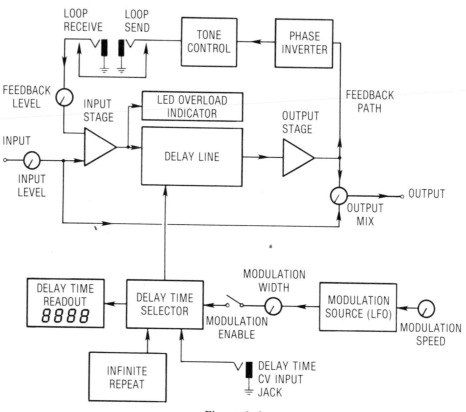

Figure 1–1

Input Level Control

Digital delays generate a small amount of noise (hiss). Since the signal-to-noise ratio represents the amount of *signal* going through a unit compared to the *noise* generated by the unit, feeding in the highest signal level possible (short of distortion) will give the best signal-to-noise ratio. Delays include an input level control (also called input, input gain, sensitivity, in) to vary the amount of signal going into the delay. For weaker signals, turn up the input control to put more signal through the delay. With a stronger signal that overloads the delay, turn down the input control to prevent distortion.

Inexpensive delay lines usually include a single LED to indicate an overload condition. If this LED lights up frequently, decrease the input level somewhat. If the LED seldom lights, then increase the input level to insure that you are sending the maximum possible signal into the delay. More costly delays often use multiple LEDs (like the LED VU meters on newer cassette recorders) to indicate not just when you have hit the overload point, but also how close you are to approaching that point.

Most rack-mount digital delays are not really designed to handle relatively weak input signals (microphone, unpreamped electric guitar, some electromechanical pianos). Attempting to use one of these signal sources will not damage the delay or instrument but might dull the sound, increase noise, or cause strange whistling effects which seem to come and go on a random basis. Should you encounter these problems, insert a preamp, compressor, or other active electronic circuit between the instrument output and delay line input. This buffers the instrument from the delay and gives a cleaner sound.

For each application, we will assume that you have correctly set the input level control for your particular combination of instrument and delay line.

Delay Time Selection

Many delays use a two-step process to select the initial delay time. (Note: We say *initial delay* because the delay time often changes during the course of certain applications.) Step 1 sets the approximate delay range with a rotary switch, set of pushbutton switches, or similar switched control. Step 2 selects the exact delay time with a continuously variable *fine delay control* (also called *delay factor* or *sweep*), which varies the delay within the range selected during Step 1.

Note, however, that there are many variations on this theme. Some delays use six pushbuttons to select six different delay ranges, along with a fine delay control; another delay might use a six-position rotary switch instead of the pushbuttons. Other delays might use fewer pushbuttons, where pushing in different *combinations* of buttons gives different ranges (i.e., with two buttons labelled A and B you could choose four possible delay ranges: pressing A by itself, pressing B by itself, pressing both A and B, or pressing neither switch).

Some delays do not use a range switch or fine delay control, but instead simply include two pushbuttons. Holding down one button increases the delay time, while holding down the other button decreases delay time. Still other delays use a calculator-type keypad to select the delay time. Delays which use these latter two methods for delay time selection often include a *delay time readout* (described later in more detail) to display the selected delay time in *milliseconds* (abbreviated ms; 1 ms = 1/1000 of a second). The owner's manual for your particular delay will describe in detail how to select different delay times.

IMPORTANT

Each application, when describing what delay time to select, specifies an *initial delay*. If your delay uses a range selector switch (or switches), choose the range that includes the time specified for initial delay. Example: Suppose your delay has three ranges (1–4 ms, 4–16 ms, and 16–64 ms). If an application specifies a 25 ms initial delay, choose the 16–64 ms range since 25 ms falls within that range. Use the fine delay control to zero in on the exact setting (unless the application specifies otherwise). Note that the calibrations on fine delay controls are often quite linear; in other words, if fine delay covers from 4 to 16 ms, the half-way point will probably be very close to 8 ms. This helps make delay time estimates more accurate.

If your delay uses dual pushbuttons to select delay time and has no fine delay control, use the pushbuttons to select the specified initial delay time and ignore any instructions about the fine delay control.

One delay line model, the Effectron I, includes a control which when turned left of center provides the fine delay function, and when turned right of center adds modulation (described next). This means that you can add modulation only at the top (minimum delay) of the delay range currently specified by the delay range setting switches. For applications which do not require modulation, treat this control as a fine delay control. For applications that do require modulation, bear in mind that you will be able to add modulation only at the minimum delay setting of a given delay range; select the delay range that gives a minimum delay time closest to the delay time specified in the application.

Modulation Speed and Modulation Width Controls

Some of the most popular delay line applications (such as chorusing) require delay times which vary slightly rather than being fixed to one specific delay time. This process of varying the delay time is called *modulation* (or *sweeping*), and imparts a more animated sound than that given by a simple fixed delay. The modulation speed control (also called LFO speed, after a circuit called a *Low Frequency Oscillator* that provides the actual modulation signal) varies the modulation rate, typically from a very slow speed (say, one cycle every 10 seconds or so) to a faster speed around 10 to 20 Hz (the general modulation speed range associated with vibrato).

The modulation width control (also called *modulation depth, LFO width*, or *LFO depth*) varies the extent to which the modulation affects the delay time. With little width, the modulation effect is subtle; with greater width, the modulation effect becomes more pronounced because it is sweeping the delay time over a wider range.

Different delays offer different maximum sweep ranges. One way to measure sweep range is to take the maximum and minimum delay times swept by the modulation in a given range, and divide the maximum delay time by the minimum delay time. Example: If at maximum width the modulation section sweeps the delay from 4 ms to 1 ms, then the delay line has a 4:1 sweep range. If at maximum depth the modulation section sweeps the delay from 32 ms to 4 ms, then the delay has an 8:1 sweep range (32/4 = 8/1).

Practically speaking, wide sweep ranges are most useful for flanging since the wider the sweep range, the more dramatic the flanging effect. However, no matter how limited the sweep range, it will be adequate at longer delays (greater than 20 ms or so) because adding any more than just a little bit of modulation at long delays usually causes detuning effects.

Feedback (Regeneration) Control

This control feeds a variable amount of the delay's output signal back into the input. For example, when using the delay as an echo unit, turning up feedback increases the number of echoes, since every time an echo arrives at the delay line output, it is sent back to the input and re-echoed.

If the feedback level is set so that the signal being fed back is weaker than the output signal, the echoes will eventually fade out since each succeeding echo will be weaker in level. If the feedback signal is the exact same level as the output, the echoes will continue at pretty much the same level. If the feedback signal is stronger than the output signal, then each echo will be stronger than the preceding echo and eventually these echoes will build up until *runaway feedback* occurs and all you hear is a mass of distortion and noise. To prevent this situation, most delays are calibrated at the factory so that the feedback control will always send back a signal whose level is less than, or equal to, the output signal.

So far we have mentioned only how this control affects echo sounds; however, adding feedback also affects flanging and chorusing effects by imparting a sharper, metallic, more resonant timbre to the flanged or chorused sound.

Feedback Phase

The feedback phase switch is most useful with short delay effects (principally flanging and chorusing). In-phase (positive) feedback gives a more metallic flanged sound, while out-of-phase (negative) feedback gives a hollower, whooshing sound. Some delays use a feedback phase control instead of a switch. Turning this control clockwise from center increases positive feedback, while turning it counterclockwise from center increases negative feedback (center position gives no feedback).

At longer delays, out-of-phase feedback can sometimes interact negatively with your straight signal and produce a thinner sound. With long echoes, always choose in-phase feedback.

Output Mix Control

The output mix control sets the mix of straight and delayed sounds. Many output mix controls are designed so that turning the control fully counterclockwise gives 100 percent straight sound, while turning it clockwise decreases the straight sound and increases the delayed sound. At midpoint, the two signals are at equal strength, and at the fully clockwise position, the output consists entirely of the delayed sound. Other delay lines use two separate controls, one to set the straight sound level and the other the delayed level. The advantage of this approach is that you can regulate the overall volume as well as set a mix of the two signals; the disadvantage is that it's more difficult to adjust two controls than a single control.

Bypass Switch

This lets you choose between the straight sound and whatever effect you have set up on the delay line (flanging, echo, doubling, and so on). Most delays include a jack on the back for plugging in a remote bypass footswitch; this feature is useful when your hands are occupied yet you want to add the delay effect selectively to different parts of a composition.

ADVANCED DELAY LINE FEATURES

Here are some features found on more sophisticated units:

Delay Time Readout

This indicates the exact delay time in milliseconds on a calculator-like numeric readout. While you might think this is a frill with little musical usefulness, you will find readouts very useful if you use echo effects related to a song's tempo. If, after finding the right echo time by trial-and-error, you note the readout reading, then it's easy to dial up that same echo time (*tempo*) at a later date. Or, if you want to make a quick half-time or double-time change, simply multiply or divide the reading by two to determine the new setting. Delay time readouts are also educational, since you learn to associate different sound effects with specific delay times.

Infinite Repeat (also called Infinite Hold)

Many delays let you record (*sample*) a sound in the delay's memory at the touch of a button, then repeat that captured section of sound indefinitely. The sampled sound can usually be as long as the delay line's maximum delay time. In some cases, once the sound is stored you can vary the pitch with the delay control or modulate it with the LFO over the same range as the delay's sweep range. If you're into electronic sounds and special effects, you can have a lot of fun with infinite repeat.

Extended Delay Time

Some models give extremely long delays—up to 4, 6, or even 8 seconds. While this may not seem all that useful now, later on in this handbook we'll describe how long delays can create solid-state tape loops, *Frippertronic* guitar techniques, and spacey sound effects.

Delay Time Control Voltage Input Jack

This is where synthesizer technology meets the delay line. Feeding a voltage into this jack controls the delay time; *increasing* the voltage typically *decreases* delay time. Thus, delay time can be controlled by footpedals, synthesizers, and other control voltage sources instead of from the front panel. Chapter 8 describes several applications that make good use of the control voltage input.

Modulation Enable Switch

This lets you switch modulation in and out remotely, and is often paralleled with a rear panel footswitch jack. Modulation enable allows for such effects as selectively adding a flanging sweep to certain phrases or chords.

Feedback Path Tone Control or High-cut Switch

Several delays now include high-cut tone controls in the feedback path so that each echo can have a little less treble than the echo immediately preceding it. By making later echoes sound duller than earlier echoes, this type of response more closely resembles natural acoustic echo where high frequencies are more readily absorbed than lower frequencies. For more information on this effect, see Application 14.

Rear Panel Feedback Path Loop Jacks

This is a more general-purpose approach to changing the feedback loop response than the one given above. Plugging an effect into these jacks breaks the delay line's feedback path and routes the feedback through the effect. Therefore, you could insert a high-cut filter to simulate the effects mentioned in the previous paragraph, or add phase shifters, delay lines, pitch transposers, and so on, for really unusual effects. Chapter 5 gives several suggestions on how to best use these jacks.

Sync (Clock) Output

This feature synchronizes electronic drums to delay time by feeding a clock signal into the drum unit's external clock input. (This input accepts a synchronizing signal which, when it is selected instead of the drum unit's normal tempo control, determines the drum unit tempo.) Most delay line clock outputs are designed so that the delay time equals one measure of the electronic drums. Thus, if the delay line is set to give one second of delay, then drums will be synchronized so that one measure equals one second. This produces extremely tight, rhythmically precise echoes. Chapters 6 and 7 describe applications that use a delay line's clock output.

Programmability

Programmable delay lines store your favorite control settings in memory; simply punch a button to recall a particular effect. (Since a delay line lets you get *lots* of different effects, it's convenient to be able to just punch up Chorus 2 or Flange 1 or whatever.) Naturally, you pay extra for this privilege. Programmable units save confusion in live performance and save time in the studio.

*   *   *   *   *

One final note about controls: Do not necessarily consider them as set-and-forget devices. Vary feedback rhythmically, change modulation speed in time with the music, change delay in the middle of a drum solo—the only way you will discover new sounds is to be creative.

*   *   *   *   *

STANDARD PATCHES

A *patch* describes how individual modules of an audio system hook together to provide a particular function. Many of the applications use the same basic patch; **Figure 1–2** shows the five standard patches (A, B, C, D, and E) that are referred to throughout the various applications.

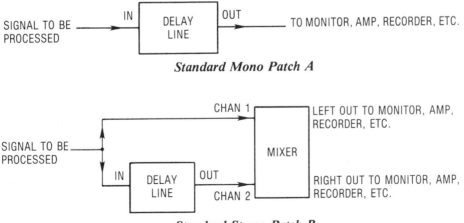

Standard Mono Patch A

Standard Stereo Patch B

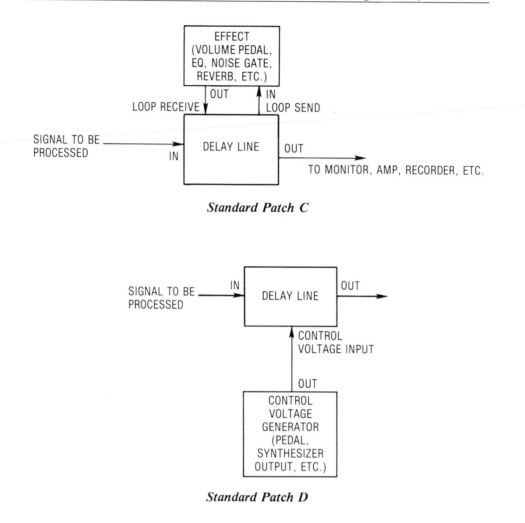

Standard Patch C

Standard Patch D

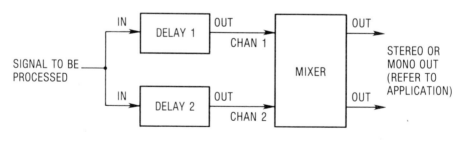

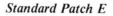

Standard Patch E

Chapter 2

Short Delay Line Applications

1 MANUAL FLANGING

Background

Flanging imparts a whooshing, jet airplane-like effect to complex sounds such as fuzz guitar, keyboards, and *program material* (i.e., entire songs or submixes of multiple tracks). Flanging can also give a sense of pitch to complex unpitched sounds (such as cymbals, snare drum, and white noise). Flanging is not as dramatic with simpler sounds (acoustic guitar, voice, and so on).

This book presents several applications of flanging. Manual flanging lets you control the flanging sweep by hand; for musicians who keep both hands occupied, Application 2 describes automatic flanging (which varies the flange sweep at a set rate), while Application 52 describes pedal flanging (which replaces the manual sweep control with a footpedal).

The Patch

See standard mono patch A.

Control Settings

The following control settings are a suggested point of departure; be sure to experiment. If you have not already done so, be sure to read the note about setting the delay time controls (entitled "Important") in Chapter 1.

Initial Delay. The flanging range extends from as short a delay as possible down to around 10 to 20 ms; 3 to 5 ms is a good place to start.

Fine Delay. Manually varying this control varies the flanging effect. (If your delay does not have a fine delay control, it will generally not be

possible to do manual flanging unless you add some custom circuitry.)
Feedback (Regeneration). This control determines the intensity of the flanging effect. Initially add about 50 percent feedback.
Feedback Phase. This determines the effect's tonality. Positive feedback gives a zingy and metallic sound while negative feedback gives a whooshing and hollow sound.
Modulation Width. Set for minimum modulation.
Modulation Speed. It does not matter with minimum modulation.
Output Mix. For the most noticeable effect, select 50 percent straight and 50 percent delayed sound.

Tweaking the Patch

For a more intense effect, increase feedback. For a less intense effect, decrease feedback. When set close to maximum feedback, some delays sound best with output mix set at 100 percent delayed sound.

You may also vary the effect's intensity with the output mix control. Example: If you like lots of feedback but find the overall sound is too shrill, increase the amount of straight signal to make the effect sound less prominent. (Any time you want a less intense flanging sound, mix in more *straight* sound with the output mix control).

Generally, delays should have a wide sweep range to provide the best possible flanging effect. However, many digital delay lines have restricted sweep ranges, which restrict the width of the available sweep. For example, with a 4:1 sweep, it will be impossible to cover the full flanging range of 0 ms to 20 ms; therefore, you will be able to sweep only a portion of the flanging range. (You could choose to sweep from, say, 1 ms to 4 ms to cover the spaciest sounding portion of the flanging range, or sweep from 5 ms to 20 ms to cover a more resonant-sounding section.) Experiment with different initial delay settings to see which portion of the flanging range sounds best to you.

2 AUTOMATIC FLANGING

Background

Automatically sweeping the flanging effect frees your hands from having to vary the fine delay control (although a disadvantage of automatic flanging is that the flange effect will not necessarily be synchronized with your playing). As with manual flanging, delay lines having a wide sweep range (at least 8:1) give the best results.

The Patch

See standard mono patch A.

Control Settings

The control settings are more crucial than for manual flanging.

Initial Delay. Select a delay in the flanging range (approximately 0 to 20 ms).

Fine Delay. Set for the widest sweep range described in your owner's manual. If there is none, experiment with this patch and note which setting of the fine delay control produces the widest sweep.

Feedback (Regeneration), Feedback Phase. See Manual Flanging (Application 1).

Modulation Width. Set for 100 percent width.

Modulation Speed. Initially set for a relatively slow sweep (i.e., one cycle every 4 or 5 seconds, or 0.2 Hz; if the modulation speed control is not calibrated, set it about one-third of the way up for now).

Output Mix. Initially select 50 percent straight and 50 percent delayed sound.

Tweaking the Patch

Most of the same advice for manual flanging applies to automatic flanging, although you will probably not vary the fine delay control once you have determined how to set it for the widest possible sweep range.

In some applications, the cyclic sound changes caused by automatic flanging may sound too regular and mechanical. If so, either vary the modulation speed control manually to help randomize the sound, or see Application 62.

3 ROTATING SPEAKER SIMULATION

Background

Some popular organs use rotating speaker systems to create timbral changes; as the speaker rotates, the listener hears reflected and direct sounds in various proportions. Delay lines can simulate the rotating speaker effect.

The Patch

See standard mono patch A.

Control Settings

The settings are similar to flanging, but are adjusted for a more subtle effect.

Initial Delay. Set for approximately 10 ms.

Feedback (Regeneration). Adjust for minimum feedback.

Feedback Phase. It does not matter with minimum feedback.

Modulation Width. Turn up just enough to hear the modulation (about 20 percent of the way up).

Modulation Speed. Initially set for a fairly fast rate (i.e., 7 to 10 Hz).

Output Mix. Select 50 percent straight and 50 percent delayed sound.

Tweaking the Patch

The modulation width control is crucial—don't turn it up too far, or the effect will not be sufficiently subtle.

Rotating speaker systems generally offer both fast and slow rotation speeds. However, when switching from one speed to another, the rate accelerates to the faster speed or decelerates to the slower speed due to the mechanical inertia of the motor system. Therefore, for the most accurate rotating speaker simulation, turn modulation speed slowly to change from one modulation rate to another.

4 VIBRATO

Background

Vibrato is a cyclic pitch change, such as occurs when you fret a guitar string and rhythmically rock your finger back and forth in a sideways motion.

The Patch

See standard mono patch A.

Control Settings

Vibrato is similar to flanging or rotating speaker simulation, except that the output mix is set for 100 percent delayed sound.
Initial Delay. Initially select a 10 ms delay.
Feedback (Regeneration). Select minimum feedback.
Feedback Phase. It does not matter with minimum feedback.
Modulation Width. Turn up about 15 percent of the way.
Modulation Speed. Select a reasonably fast speed in the vibrato range (7 to 14 Hz).
Output Mix. Select 100 percent delayed sound.

Tweaking the Patch

The initial delay setting can influence the vibrato's *smoothness*. Therefore, after setting the desired amount of modulation width and speed, see if changing the initial delay can improve the sound. Some readjustment of the modulation controls may also be necessary.

Occasionally, the modulation width control may be so sensitive that turning the control up by even a small amount will produce too pronounced a vibrato. Should this occur, you can often decrease the modulation sensitivity by shortening the initial delay.

Also note that you can selectively vibrato particular chords or notes by switching (via the bypass switch) between the delayed and straight sounds.

5 PHASE SHIFTER SIMULATION

Background

Phase shifters, introduced in the early 70s, were intended to simulate the sound of tape flanging. However, since these devices did not use true time delay technology, they produced a subtler effect than true flanging. While flanging and phase shifting sound quite different, it is possible to simulate a typical phase shifter sound with a digital delay line.

The Patch

See standard mono patch A.

Control Settings

The control settings are similar to those for flanging, but this application sweeps a much narrower portion of the short delay range.
Initial Delay. Set for approximately 2 ms.
Feedback (Regeneration). Initially select minimum feedback (see *Tweaking the Patch*).
Feedback Phase. Select negative phase.
Modulation Width. Add about 50 percent modulation.
Modulation Speed. Adjust to suit yourself—start off at a medium rate.
Output Mix. Select 50 percent straight and 50 percent delayed sound.

Tweaking the Patch

Since phase shifters are generally characterized by short delay times and fairly narrow sweep ranges, play with the initial delay and modulation width controls for the best results. Wide sweep range delays will require particularly low modulation width control settings.

For a sharper sound, turn up feedback somewhat (negative feedback seems to give the most realistic phase shifter sound).

6 TONE CONTROL (COMB FILTER)

Background

Mixing a straight signal with the *same* signal passed through a short delay produces a filtering effect that changes the signal's tone. This type of filter is called a *comb filter* since plotting its frequency response looks somewhat like a comb (see **Figure 2-1**).

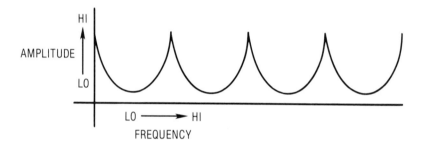

Figure 2-1

The Patch

See standard mono patch A.

Control Settings

Generally, tone control patches use the delay's short delay range and include no modulation.

Initial Delay. Select a delay time around 2 or 3 ms.

Fine Delay. Vary to change the tone quality of the signal being processed.

Feedback (Regeneration). Initially select minimum feedback.

Feedback Phase. See *Tweaking the Patch*.

Modulation Width. Select minimum modulation.

Modulation Speed. It does not matter with minimum modulation.

Output Mix. Set for 50 percent straight and 50 percent delayed sound.

Tweaking the Patch

Experiment! Increasing initial delay out to about 10 ms noticeably varies the tone control's effect. Increasing feedback creates a more resonant sound by accenting the filter peaks and dips. For yet another type of sound, change feedback phase from positive to negative; this reverses the positions of the frequency response peaks and valleys.

With lots of feedback, the overall sound might be too sharp. Should this be a problem, set the output mix control for more straight sound and less delayed sound; this places the whistling, resonant effect more in the background.

7 CHORUSING

Background

Chorusing, an extremely popular effect, thickens the sound of an instrument in a way that resembles instruments playing *en ensemble*. The optimum initial delay for chorusing extends from about 10 ms to 25 ms; longer delays give a thicker chorus sound, while shorter delays give an effect which sounds more like a cross between flanging and chorusing.

The Patch

See standard mono patch A.

Control Settings

Subtlety is important when chorusing, so vary the controls slowly and carefully.

Initial Delay. Select a 10 to 25 ms initial delay.

Feedback (Regeneration). Add about 25 percent feedback.

Feedback Phase. Select positive feedback.

Modulation Width. Turn up slightly; turning up too much can create an out-of-tune effect.

Modulation Speed. Generally, a relatively slow speed gives you the most majestic sound.

Output Mix. Set for 50 percent straight and 50 percent delayed sound.

Tweaking the Patch

This is a fairly critical effect to get just right. Generally, the slower the modulation speed, the more you can turn up modulation width. Combining slow modulation speed with substantial modulation width produces a wide-range, full-sounding chorus effect. Random modulation (if available) will give a less predictable chorusing sound that helps reinforce the ensemble illusion.

The initial delay setting is also important. If you hear a discrete echo, then the initial delay time is probably too long. Alternately, if the effect sounds more like flanging than chorusing, the delay is probably too short. Many musicians prefer to set as long a delay as possible short of hearing an obvious echo effect, and use fairly narrow modulation width. Adjust to suit yourself.

For a more metallic chorus sound, turn up feedback. If the chorus effect dominates too much, use the output mix control to add more straight sound and less delayed sound.

8 DOUBLING

Background.

In the studio, musicians often play a part and then play the *same* part as an overdub. Combining the two parts together creates a bigger sound than a single part. However, there will usually be slight timing differences between the two overdubs (no player can duplicate a part *exactly*), which creates a pseudo-random, tight echo effect.

The Patch

See standard mono patch A.

Control Settings

As with most short delay applications, the settings are rather critical.
Initial Delay. Select an initial delay around 25 ms—just long enough to hear a noticeable, but not obvious, echo.
Feedback (Regeneration). Select minimum feedback.
Feedback Phase. It does not matter with minimum feedback.
Modulation Width. Turn up about 20 percent to subtly change the echo time.
Modulation Speed. Set for a fairly slow speed.
Output Mix. Initially set for 50 percent straight and 50 percent delayed sound; adjust later if necessary.

Tweaking the Patch

Initial delay is the most crucial control for doubling—it must be long enough to create a doubling effect, yet not so long that you hear an obvious echo.

The modulation controls also require some attention since they animate the overall sound to prevent it from becoming too static. For best results, set modulation speed for a fairly slow sweep and add modulation width sparingly.

9 BATHTUB REVERB

Background

This has also been called *hard reverb*, *cardboard tube reverb*, and several other names. The end result is the same: the type of reverb you experience in a small space with extremely hard surfaces.

The Patch

See standard mono patch A.

Control Settings

Although many of these settings are a matter of taste, here are some suggested starting points.
Initial Delay. Select an initial delay around 30 ms.
Feedback (Regeneration). Add about 75 percent feedback (but avoid runaway feedback).
Feedback Phase. Select positive feedback.
Modulation Width. Set for minimum modulation.
Modulation Speed. It does not matter with minimum modulation.
Output Mix. Initially set for 50 percent straight and 50 percent delayed sound.

Tweaking the Patch

This gimmicky reverb sound lends itself to being made as gimmicky as possible. If you get tired of sci-fi effects, either pull back on the feedback control somewhat or dial in more straight sound with the output mix control.

Incidentally, a tiny bit of modulation at a medium modulation speed can add some shimmer to the basic sound.

10 HALL REVERB

Background

While a single delay line cannot give true concert hall reverb effects, this patch is about as close as you can come. It is especially effective when patched before a standard digital or analog reverb unit (see **Figure 2-2**).

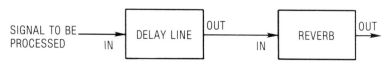

Figure 2-2

The Patch

See standard mono patch A.

Control Settings

The control settings are quite critical; expect to spend some time tweaking this patch.

Initial Delay. Select a 24 ms initial delay.

Feedback (Regeneration). Turn up feedback as far as possible, short of runaway feedback.

Feedback Phase. Select positive feedback.

Modulation Width. Turn up about 10 percent of the way.

Modulation Speed. Set for slowest modulation speed.

Output Mix. Initially set for 50 percent straight and 50 percent delayed sound.

Tweaking the Patch

The initial delay setting is very important: you should hear individual echoes which are spaced so closely together that they appear like a continuous stream of sound. Too short a delay produces a tonal feeling, while too long a delay sounds more like the bathtub reverb described in Application 9.

For a more natural effect, add a barely noticeable amount of modulation and use the output mix control to favor the straight sound. Also experiment with the feedback control; less feedback softens the room surfaces. Finally, restricting the feedback path's high frequency response (see Application 14) will give a more life-like sound.

Chapter 3

Echo Applications

~~~~~~

11 50s-STYLE SLAPBACK ECHO

Background

In the early days of recording, echo effects were provided by tape recorders rather than by the digital wonder boxes we know today. Feeding a signal into the tape recorder input, going into record, rolling tape, and monitoring the signal coming from the playback head produced a typical delay of around 70 ms. Properly setting a digital delay can replicate this echo effect.

The Patch

See standard mono patch A.

Control Settings

Initial Delay. Select a 70 ms initial delay.
Feedback (Regeneration). Start off with minimum feedback; increase later if desired.
Feedback Phase. Select positive feedback.
Modulation Width. Set for minimum modulation.
Modulation Speed. It does not matter with minimum modulation.
Output Mix. Set for about 60 percent straight sound, 40 percent delayed sound.

Tweaking the Patch

Experiment with turning up the feedback and varying the output mix.

12 REVERB PRE-DELAY

+ Outboard reverberation unit, mixer.

Background

In a natural acoustic space, it takes a while for sound waves to travel through the air before hitting the walls; unfortunately, with simple reverb units the reverb sound occurs virtually immediately after receiving a signal. A digital delay can improve the reverb's realism by adding the *pre-delay* effect associated with large concert halls.

The Patch

Referring to **Figure 3-1**, send the signal being reverberated to the delay line input and one mixer input. Send the delay line output to the reverb unit input, and the reverb unit output to a second mixer input. Turning up channel 1 increases the straight level, while turning up channel 2 adds in the reverberated sound.

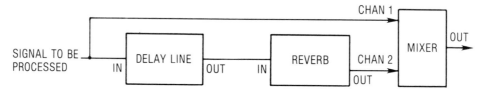

Figure 3-1

Control Settings

The settings are similar to those for doubling and slapback echo.
Initial Delay. Typical pre-delay times are 20 to 60 ms. Increasing delay time increases the size of the room.
Feedback (Regeneration). Select minimum feedback.
Feedback Phase. It does not matter with minimum feedback.
Modulation Width. Select minimum modulation width.
Modulation Speed. It does not matter with minimum modulation width.
Output Mix. Set for 100 percent delayed sound.

Tweaking the Patch

Vary the initial delay time for the best-sounding reverb effect. Too long a delay will create an unnatural sound, while too short a delay will not give a sufficiently noticeable pre-delay effect. To thicken as well as delay the reverb, increase the feedback control somewhat.

With stereo setups, use two delay lines for pre-delay (one for each channel), with each delay set to slightly different delay times.

13 STANDARD ECHO

Background

Echo has been a popular effect for decades. Compared to older tape echo units, digital delay lines give cleaner echo effects and require far less maintenance.

The Patch

See standard mono patch A.

Control Settings

The echo range extends from about 50 ms out to several seconds, with different times giving different psycho-acoustic effects (shorter echoes tend to sound nervous; longer echoes sound spacey).
Initial Delay. As a point of departure, start off with about 500 ms of delay.
Feedback (Regeneration). Turn feedback up about 75 percent.
Feedback Phase. Select positive feedback.
Modulation Width. Set for minimum modulation.
Modulation Speed. It does not matter with minimum modulation.
Output Mix. Initially. set for 60 percent straight and 40 percent delayed sound.

Tweaking the Patch

 The major variables are delay time and feedback. Increasing feedback increases the number of echoes, from a single echo (with minimum feedback) to lots of echoes (with 100 percent feedback). Combining long delay times and feedback gives an evocative sound. To place the delay effect further in the background, set output mix for less delayed sound.

14 NATURAL ECHO SOUND

+ Either a feedback path tone control, feedback path high-cut switch, or rear panel feedback path loop jacks (see Chapter 5) and outboard equalizer.

Background

In a natural acoustic space, echoes lose high frequencies faster than low frequencies; thus, each successive echo sounds duller than previous echoes. Since digital delay lines have excellent frequency response, successive echoes all sound pretty much alike — which does not really simulate the sound of an echo in an acoustic space. Restricting the feedback signal's frequency response more closely approximates a natural echo sound by decreasing an echo's treble every time it passes through the feedback path.

The Patch

If the delay line includes either a tone control or high-cut switch in the feedback path, then this application uses standard mono patch A. If the delay line does not include a tone control or switch but does include rear panel feedback path loop jacks, patch an external equalizer (graphic, parametric, or with similar tone control) into these jacks as shown in standard patch C. For more information on using delay line loop jacks, see Chapter 5.

Control Settings

Control settings are similar to the ones for standard echo (Application 13), with the following exceptions:
Initial Delay. Start off at 100 ms or so.
Feedback Path Tone Control or High-cut Switch (if present). Set for reduced high frequency response.
Rear Panel Feedback Path Loop Jacks (if present). After patching in an equalizer, set it for reduced high frequency response.

Tweaking the Patch.

Choose a moderate amount of feedback. For the most natural sound, set the output mix control for mostly straight sound and keep the delayed sound in the background. Also, since natural acoustic spaces have finite boundaries, you may want to avoid using outrageously long echo times.

15 ECHO WITH CHORUSING

Background

To add chorusing to echo effects, simply turn up the modulation width control by a very small amount. Although it is difficult to set the modulation controls under these conditions (you have to wait for an echo in order to hear the effects of any control setting changes), carefully adjusting modulation can yield a good echo-with-chorus sound.

The Patch

See standard mono patch A.

Control Settings

Adjust all controls as you would for standard echo (Application 13), with the following exceptions:

Modulation Width. Turn up very, very slightly and temporarily play a continuous sound such as a chord on a guitar or taped down keys on a keyboard. As echoes occur, you should hear effects that are similar to flanging and chorusing. Generally, you will not want to turn this control up too far, since an excessive amount of pitch-shifting will give an out-of-tune feeling.

Modulation Speed. Slow speeds tend to work best as they create the least amount of pitch-shifting.

Tweaking the Patch

As with traditional chorusing, the slower the modulation speed, the more the modulation width can be turned up.

16 SYNCHRO-SONIC ECHO EFFECTS

+ Delay time readout feature (optional; see text).

Background.

At longer echo times, synchronizing the echo time to the tempo of the music being played gives a more rhythmically cohesive (*synchro-sonic*) feeling. The problem is to find out what delay time will sync with the tempo of the music. However, if you know the tempo of a song in beats-per-minute you can easily calculate a suitable delay time (as explained below). After converting a song's tempo from beats-per-minute into milliseconds-per-measure, you may then set the echo time for a multiple or submultiple of the measure time.

The Formula

The following formula converts beats-per-minute into milliseconds-per-measure:

(60/(BPM/TS)) x 1000 = milliseconds per measure, where BPM is the tempo in beats-per-minute and TS is the numerator of the time signature (i.e., TS = 4 for 4/4, 5 for 5/4, 7 for 7/4, and so on).

Example: Suppose a song's tempo is 120 beats per minute and the time signature is 4/4. Plugging this into our formula, we get:

(60/(120/4)) × 1000 = (60/30) × 1000 = 2 × 1000 = 2000 milliseconds (2 seconds) per measure.

Once we know the time per measure, it's easy to calculate echo times for quarter notes, half notes, and so on. Since an echo time of one measure (one whole note) equals 2 seconds, then:

A half-note echo time would equal 1 second. A quarter-note echo time would equal 500 ms. An eighth-note echo time would equal 250 ms. A sixteenth-note echo time would equal 125 ms.

Thus, with a 250 ms echo time, the echo will occur one eighth note after the original signal. Turning up the feedback control will produce a series of echoes spaced one eighth note apart.

While the above makes it easy to determine synchro-sonic echo times, you need to know the tempo of a song in beats-per-minute and you need a delay line with a readout as well. The following variation gives acceptable synchronization effects without needing to know the precise tempo or delay time.

The Patch

See standard mono patch A.

Control Settings

Initial Delay. Initially set for about 250 ms.
Fine Delay. Vary as described under *Tweaking the Patch.*
Feedback (Regeneration). Add about 50 percent feedback.
Feedback Phase. Select positive feedback.
Modulation Width. Select minimum modulation.
Modulation Speed. It does not matter with minimum modulation.
Output Mix. Set for 50 percent straight and 50 percent delayed sound.

Tweaking the Patch

While listening to the song to which you want to synchronize, play a sharp sound (such as a drum beat, quickly strummed guitar chord, or fast-decay synthesizer tone) through the delay line and note the timing of the echoes with respect to the rhythm of the song. If the echoes *lead* the song's tempo (i.e., the echoes occur too close together), lengthen the initial delay time. If the echoes *lag* the song's tempo (i.e., they occur too far apart), shorten the delay.

As you adjust the fine delay control, the echoes will start to repeat in time with the music. Next, turn up feedback as far as possible to hear more repeats, and adjust the delay control for as close a sync as possible between echo and tempo. Continue tweaking the initial delay until the echoes are synchronized with the song.

After determining the correct delay time, reduce the feedback for a more conventional sound (unless, of course, you like all those echoes).

17 PSEUDO PITCH CHANGED ECHO

Background

Application 34 describes how patching a pitch transposer into the delay's loop jacks can create echoes that spiral upward or downward in pitch. This application produces a similar effect but does not require any additional equipment.

The Patch

See standard mono patch A.

Control Settings

Initial Delay. Select an initial delay of 250 ms.
Feedback (Regeneration). Add at least 75 percent feedback.
Feedback Phase. Select positive feedback.
Modulation Width. Select 100 percent width.
Modulation Speed. Set for slowest speed.
Output Mix. Set for 60 percent straight and 40 percent delayed sound.

Tweaking the Patch

Strike a single note; it will echo at the rate set by the initial delay, but as the modulation goes through its cycle the pitch will shift either up or down. Modulation width determines the total amount of pitch shift. Unlike Application 35, you have no control over the pitch shift direction; it depends entirely on whether the modulation LFO is rising or falling.

18 SELECTIVELY ADDED ECHOES

+ Outboard mixer, volume pedal.

Background

This application describes how to add echoes to a specific note or group of notes rather than to all notes being played.

The Patch

Figure 3–2 shows the required connections for this patch. Note that the footpedal must be inserted before, not after, the delay line.

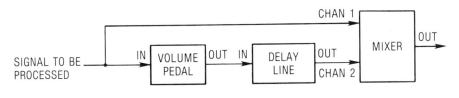

Figure 3–2

Control Settings

Refer to previous echo applications (such as Application 13) for information on how to set the various controls; however, for this application, set the output mix for 100 percent delayed sound. Turn up mixer channel 1 to hear the straight instrument sound and mixer channel 2 to hear the echo. (Note: If adding in channel 2 produces a thinner sound, change the channel 2 phase reversal switch.)

Tweaking the Patch

After setting up the patch, press down on the pedal so that you can hear the echoes, then adjust the delay line controls for the desired echo effect. Next, lift back on the pedal and wait for the echoes to fade out.

To selectively add echo to one note, increase the footpedal volume just *before* the note begins and decrease the footpedal volume just *after* the note ends. To echo an entire phrase, push down on the pedal before the phrase begins and pull back just after the phrase ends.

19 FRIPPERTRONIC ECHO EFFECTS

+ Extended delay time (at least 3 or 4 seconds).

Background

This style of playing, popularized by British guitarist Robert Fripp, requires very long echo times. Before the advent of long delay lines, composers used two tape recorders to create extremely long echoes by recording a signal at the record head of one recorder, then threading the tape through a second recorder and picking up the signal from the second recorder's playback head (see **Figure 3-3**). As you might imagine, this is a somewhat iffy technique—the tape can get fouled, and tape recorders were never really designed for this application. Nowadays, it is far more convenient to use long digital delays in place of dual tape recorders.

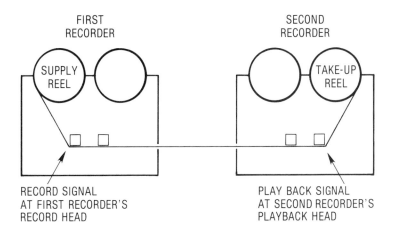

Figure 3-3

The Patch

See standard mono patch A.

Control Settings

Control settings for this patch are highly subjective, but here are some suggested starting points.

Initial Delay. Set for at least 3 seconds of delay.

Feedback (Regeneration). Adjust for maximum feedback (short of runaway feedback).

Feedback Phase. Select positive feedback.

Modulation Width. Select minimum modulation.

Modulation Speed. It does not matter with minimum modulation.

Output Mix. Set for 50 percent straight and 50 percent delayed sounds.

Tweaking the Patch

This patch requires some specialized playing techniques. For best results, play either long sustaining notes or clusters of repetitive notes. Example: Play the tonic of a chord and let that repeat; play the third and let that repeat; then play the fifth and let that repeat. All three notes will now be echoing and feeding back to create a chord. At this point, either continue playing over the repeating chord to create an even thicker texture, or store the chord by using the infinite repeat feature (see Application 24) and play a lead on top of the repeating chord sound.

This patch is highly level-sensitive, so you may have to re-adjust the input level control periodically to prevent distortion.

20 CANON ECHO

Background

A canon is a type of musical composition in which the same melody is played or sung by two or more voice parts (probably the best-known examples are *Row, Row, Row Your Boat* and *Frère Jacques*). A delay line can give a simplified version of this effect by delaying what you play, then repeating it a fraction of a second later.

The Patch

See standard mono patch A.

Control Settings

Initial Delay. Set for the desired time interval between the time you start playing and the time the second part should start playing (see *Tweaking the Patch* for a practical example).
Feedback (Regeneration). Select minimum feedback (single repeat).
Feedback Phase. It does not matter with minimum feedback.
Modulation Width. Select minimum modulation.
Modulation Speed. It does not matter with minimum modulation.
Output Mix. Set for 50 percent straight and 50 percent delayed sounds.

Tweaking the Patch

The following example illustrates how to use this technique. Set the echo time for a *half-note* echo (see Application 16). Now, play a major scale in a *quarter-note* rhythm. The delay line will play back whatever you play into it with a half-note lag, thus creating harmonies with the notes you are playing. The delay time should be synchronized with the tempo of the piece.

To mix the harmony line more in the background, set output mix for less delayed sound. If desired, you can add vibrato to the harmony line with the modulation controls.

Chapter 4

Special Effects

21 ROBOT VOICES (VOCODER SIMULATION)

Background

Sci-fi films often use a *vocoder* (an expensive signal processor) to create mechanical-sounding robot voices. Speaking through a properly adjusted digital delay line can give you a similar effect (although, of course, a digital delay cannot simulate other vocoder effects).

The Patch

This application uses standard mono patch A. Feed a microphone into the delay line input.

Control Settings

The settings for this patch are quite critical, so be prepared to experiment.
Initial Delay. Set a 15 to 20 ms initial delay.
Feedback (Regeneration). Turn feedback up as far as possible, short of runaway feedback.
Feedback Phase. Select positive feedback.
Modulation Width. Set for minimum modulation.
Modulation Speed. It does not matter with minimum modulation.
Output Mix. Set for 100 percent delayed sound.

Tweaking the Patch

As you speak into the microphone, vary the delay time until your voice acquires a suitably metallic timbre.

One popular vocoder effect is to change the pitch of the vocoder signal; to imitate this effect with a delay line, vary the delay time. Unfortunately, this method usually precludes rapid, accurate pitch selection. A better alternative, assuming that the delay line has a delay time control voltage (CV) input, is to feed a synthesizer keyboard CV output into the delay line CV input so that you can play the delay time from the keyboard. See Application 56 for more information on this technique.

22 SIMPLE PITCH SHIFTING

Background

Varying the delay time while feeding a sound into the delay shifts the sound's pitch for as long as the delay time is being varied. The magnitude of the pitch shift depends on the delay time; longer delays generally give greater pitch shifts.

If you stop varying the delay time, the signal returns to normal pitch (the longer the delay, the longer it takes to return to normal). Delay line pitch-shifting is particularly useful with drums and similar percussive sounds, but you can also create some fairly bizarre vocal effects.

The Patch

See standard mono patch A.

Control Settings

Unlike some delay patches where you set and forget the controls, pitch-shifting requires that you vary the delay time (usually via the fine delay) as you process the input signal. If there is no fine delay control, you will have a difficult time creating smooth pitch-shift effects.

Initial Delay. Initially select a 25 ms delay.

Fine Delay. Vary as the signal goes through the delay line. Lengthening the delay time shifts pitch downward, while shortening the delay time shifts pitch upward.

Feedback (Regeneration). Set for minimum feedback.

Feedback Phase. It does not matter with minimum feedback.

Modulation Width. Select minimum modulation.

Modulation Speed. It does not matter with minimum modulation.

Output Mix. Initially select 100 percent delayed sound.

Tweaking the Patch

For a more pronounced pitch-shifting effect, increase initial delay. To accompany the pitch-shifted sound with some straight signal, set the output mix control for more straight sound.

Increasing feedback or altering the feedback phase can produce some novel effects.

23 MONO-TO-STEREO CONVERSION (SYNTHESIZED STEREO)

+ Mixer, Y-cord or other signal splitter.

Background

Suppose that you want to record a stereo drum sound on tape, but can only record in mono due to track limitations. One solution is to record the track in mono, then use a delay line during mixdown to artificially spread the mono track into stereo.

The Patch

See standard stereo patch B. Split the input signal to one mixer channel and to the delay line input using a Y-cord or similar signal splitter. The delay line output feeds the other stereo channel.

Control Settings

This will require a fair amount of tweaking, but the following should get you started.

Initial Delay. Select an 18 ms initial delay.

Fine Delay. See *Tweaking the Patch.*

Feedback (Regeneration). Select minimum feedback.

Feedback Phase. It does not matter with minimum feedback.

Modulation Width. Set for minimum modulation.

Modulation Speed. It does not matter with minimum modulation.

Output Mix. Set for 100 percent delayed sound.

Tweaking the Patch

This is a tricky patch to apply, because combining a synthesized stereo signal back into mono (as would happen if you heard the stereo signal over, say, a mono AM radio) can sound different from the original mono signal. This problem occurs because the delay line synthesizes the additional channel by passing the straight signal through a short delay—and recombining a short-delayed signal along with a non-delayed signal can produce frequency response changes (see Application 6). Therefore, monitor the stereo sound panned to center (mono) as well as in stereo, and carefully adjust the fine delay or initial delay control for the least amount of tonal change when going back and forth between synthesized stereo and mono.

For a more unusual sound, try adding some feedback.

24 SOLID-STATE TAPE LOOP EFFECTS

+ Infinite Repeat (or Infinite Hold) feature.

Background

Many electronic music experimenters have made good compositional use of *tape loops*. To make a tape loop, you record a sound (usually of short duration) and splice the end of the taped sound back to its beginning. Thus, as you play the loop, the sound will repeat over and over and over and over and over and over and over and . . . you get the idea.

However, tape recorders were not designed to play loops, so it often requires a careful hand to guide the tape loop through the tape path. Another problem is that tape loops can break or wear out. Fortunately, digital delays can serve as *solid-state tape loops*, thus solving these problems. The only disadvantage to using a delay line is that when you turn off its power, the delay will forget whatever sound you had stored; with a tape loop, the sound remains on the loop until it is either damaged or erased.

The Patch

See standard mono patch A.

Control Settings

Initial control settings are not particularly critical, but you will have to do a fair amount of tweaking for the best possible results.
Initial Delay. Select a delay time equal to the desired loop time. (Note: A few delays cannot store *less* than their maximum amount of delay, regardless of the delay time setting.)
Infinite Repeat. Push infinite repeat just *after* the sound you want to loop has ended. Example: To loop a one second sound, set initial delay for one second and play the sound. Immediately after the sound has ended, press infinite repeat. The sound, now stored in the delay line,

will continue repeating until power is turned off.

You may also *layer* sounds by selecting maximum feedback and playing for a while. After you have built up enough layers of sound, press infinite repeat.

Fine Delay. This control transposes the stored sound. Lengthening the delay time transposes the pitch downward and increases the loop time, while shortening the delay time transposes the pitch upward and decreases the loop time (see *Tweaking the Patch*).

Feedback (Regeneration). Select minimum feedback.

Feedback Phase. It does not matter with minimum feedback.

Modulation Width. Select minimum modulation.

Modulation Speed. It does not matter with minimum modulation.

Output Mix. Set for 100 percent delayed sound.

Tweaking the Patch

There are two ways to tweak the patch: Either alter the signal as it is being recorded into the delay line, or once the sound has been stored, alter the stored sound.

Examples: To pitch-shift a sound while recording, vary the fine delay control (see Application 22). To modulate the sound while recording, add modulation.

After storing the signal in the delay line, transpose the stored sound with the fine delay control, modulate the stored sound with the modulation controls, or both transpose and modulate the stored sound. Note: Unfortunately, some delays do not allow for altering the sound once it has been stored.

25 LIVE DIGITAL MULTITRACK RECORDING

+ Extended delay feature (at least 3 or 4 seconds) and Infinite Repeat.

Background

Combining a long echo time with lots of feedback simulates multitrack recording, since when you play a musical phrase, the feedback will cause it to repeat over and over again; you may then overdub by playing new lines on top of this repeating phrase. These overdubs will repeat as well, so you can continue overdubbing parts to build up several tracks of sound (see example below), and finally select infinite repeat to store the multitracked sound. The only limitation is that until you select infinite repeat, every time a sound repeats, its fidelity deteriorates somewhat. However, you should be able to record plenty of overdubs before the sound quality becomes objectionable.

Example: If the delay time is set for the equivalent of two measures of music, you could initially play a two-measure bass line on a programmable synthesizer, then switch over to another patch and overdub a two-measure melody over the bass line. As the bass and melody continue to repeat, you could then change patches a third time and lay down yet another part. This can continue until the sound quality becomes intolerably poor, or until you have played everything that you wanted to play. After playing the parts, select infinite repeat to store the parts without any further signal degradation. You may then play along with the stored rhythm track as it repeats.

The Patch

This application uses standard mono patch A.

Control Settings

Initial Delay. Adjust the delay time to equal a measure or two (or more, if possible) of the music you are playing.

Feedback. Feedback is the most important control—it must be turned up high enough so that each successive echo maintains the same volume level as the previous echo, yet not be turned up so high that runaway feedback occurs. To set this control properly, temporarily select a fairly short delay time (i.e., 50 ms) and play a sound through the delay. Set feedback to the maximum possible setting short of runaway feedback, then return to the desired delay setting.

Feedback Phase. Always use positive feedback for this application. If you have a feedback path hi-cut control, leave it off so that the feedback signal has the greatest possible frequency response.

Modulation Width. Select minimum modulation.

Modulation Speed. It does not matter with minimum modulation.

Output Mix. Initially select 50 percent straight and 50 percent delayed sound. When playing over the repeating measure, you might want to mix the stored (repeating) sound more in the background.

Tweaking the Patch

To optimize fidelity, work rapidly while recording, and select infinite repeat as soon as possible once all sounds have been recorded. Some delays allow for modulating and transposing the stored signal with (respectively) the modulation and fine delay controls.

26 VOCAL WITH STEREO SPREAD SIBILANCE ECHO

+ Outboard equalizer (parametric, graphic, and so on), stereo mixer.

Background

When echoing voice, sometimes the echo *steps on* (tends to obscure) the main vocal. One solution is to thin out the echo sound by restricting its frequency response. Generally, cutting out the bass and echoing only the highs produces a tight, sibilance-enhancing effect that makes the vocal more prominent and intelligible. Since this patch separates the sibilance echo sound from the main vocal, you can place the echo sound anywhere in the stereo field; however, in most cases you will want to place the straight vocal in the middle of the stereo field.

The Patch

This is a variation on standard stereo patch B. **Figure 4–1** shows how to split the vocal signal through an equalizer and delay line to create the stereo spread.

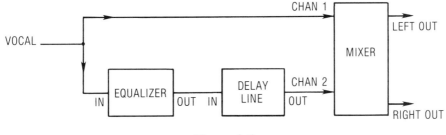

Figure 4–1

Control Settings

First, adjust the controls as you would for standard echo (Application 13) *except* set output mix for 100 percent delayed sound. Second, thin out the echo sound by adjusting the equalizer for a treble boost, bass cut, or both—whatever works best. Note that boosting the treble (rather than cutting the bass) is more likely to overload the delay line and, also, you may need to re-adjust the delay line's input level control (and possibly feedback control) for different equalizer settings.

Tweaking the Patch

Experiment with boosting and cutting various frequencies to see which sounds best with a particular voice.

27 WARPED RECORD SIMULATOR

Background

Those who do sound work for films or the theater sometimes get requests for strange sound effects. If you ever need to simulate a warped record, this is the patch.

The Patch

See standard mono patch A. Feed the sound or program material to be warped into the input.

Control Settings

Initial Delay. Set for the slapback echo range (around 50 ms).
Feedback (Regeneration). Select minimum feedback.
Feedback Phase. It does not matter with minimum feedback.
Modulation Width. Set for desired amount of warpage. The more modulation, the greater the simulated amount of warp.
Modulation Speed. To simulate a warped 33-1/3 RPM record, set the modulation speed as close as possible to 0.55 Hz. To simulate a warped 45 RPM record, set the speed to 0.75 Hz. To simulate a warped 78 RPM record, set the speed to 1.3 Hz.
Output Mix. Set for 100 percent delayed sound.

Tweaking the Patch

For more warp, increase the delay time or the modulation width.

28 OBSCENITY REMOVER FOR BROADCASTERS

+ Extended delay feature (at least 4 seconds, preferably 6 or 7 seconds) with broadcast-quality fidelity, beep generator, monitor system, switch to change signal from delay line output to beep generator.

Background

This patch is for all the musicians who work at college radio stations. Some talk shows and other live broadcasts use a delay line to preview (by several seconds) what goes out on the air. Thus, if someone tries to broadcast an obscene or libelous statement, the signal can be interrupted and replaced with a beep tone. After the problematic statement has passed, switching out the beep signal restores the normal audio.

The Patch

This patch is fairly elaborate (see **Figure 4-2**). The audio switch can be a simple mechanical switch, but if you run into clicks and pops when switching, use an electronically controlled FET switch for silent audio switching.

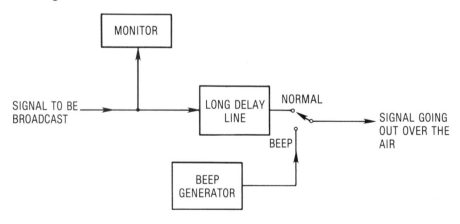

Figure 4-2

Control Settings

Settings are not overly critical. The most important consideration is to process the audio signal as cleanly as possible to maintain broadcast quality.

Initial Delay. Set for a 4 to 7 second delay.

Feedback (Regeneration). Select minimum feedback.

Feedback Phase. It does not matter with minimum feedback.

Modulation Width. Select minimum modulation.

Modulation Speed. It does not matter with minimum modulation.

Output Mix. Set for 100 percent delayed sound.

Tweaking the Patch

To use the system, monitor the *input* to the delay line (not the output). If you hear an offending statement, flick the switch to insert the beep generator into the signal path instead of the delay line output. After the offending statement has ended, wait for an amount of time equal to the delay time, then switch the delay line output back into the signal path.

29 ATTACK ELIMINATOR

+ Outboard noise gate with external trigger input, mixer.

Background

The first few milliseconds of a percussive note's attack usually contain high-level transients. While these add character to the sound, they can sometimes cause technical problems (such as tape overload). This patch removes the attack from a note and thus eliminates the initial transients. It can also help cut out *artifacts* (such as pick sounds, clicks, switch pops, and the like), provide a stereo pseudo-panning effect if you pan the straight signal to one channel and the attack-eliminated signal to the other channel, or trap transients on their way to a spring reverb input (spring reverbs do not like transients).

The Patch

Referring to **Figure 4-3**, the audio signal feeds the noise gate and delay simultaneously, but the delayed signal—not the straight signal—controls the noise gate via the external trigger input. Thus, the noise gate turns on later than the straight signal going through it.

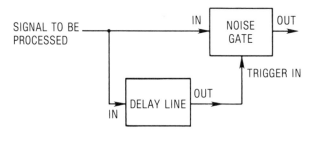

Figure 4-3

Control Settings

Initial Delay. Set for the amount of attack time to be removed (this will often be fairly short).
Feedback (Regeneration). Select minimum feedback.

Feedback Phase. It does not matter with minimum feedback.
Modulation Width. Select minimum modulation.
Modulation Speed. It does not matter with minimum modulation.
Output Mix. Set for 100 percent delayed sound.

Tweaking the Patch

For the noise gate to re-trigger with each new note attack, there must be a silence between notes equal to the delay time. Otherwise, when the next transient occurs, the delayed signal will still be keeping the noise gate turned on.

Chapter 5

Using the Delay Line Feedback Loop Jacks

～～～～～～～～～～～～～～～～～～～～

Important ————————————————————

Depending on your particular delay line, plugging into the feedback loop jacks can affect the action of the front panel feedback control in one of three ways:

1. The feedback control will become inoperative.

2. The feedback control will set the overall level of the signal going through the loop jacks.

3. The feedback control will add feedback as it normally does, without affecting any feedback added via the loop.

If the effect is (1), you needn't do anything to prepare for the applications presented in this Chapter; if the effect is (2), initially turn feedback up all the way; if the effect is (3), turn feedback down all the way. If you are not sure how your delay line works, consult the owner's manual or try one of the following applications and note how the feedback control reacts.

Most delay lines work as described in (2), so you can use the delay line's front panel feedback control to alter the amount of feedback going through the external loop. If your delay line acts as described in (1) or (3), you may need to add an external *attenuator* (level control) between the effect output and the loop receive jack to control the amount of feedback (see **Figure 5-1**). In this case, if an application mentions varying the feedback control, vary the external attenuator instead.

With most delays, any feedback loop processing will affect all echoes *after* the first echo. This is because the first echo reaches the output without being processed. As this first echo goes back through the feedback loop, it is processed and then reaches the output a second time. Thus, all echoes after the first echo are processed.

It is possible to set up feedback loop patches so that the first echo is processed as well as subsequent echoes. You will need two Y cords and a mixer. Split the instrument output; send one signal line to the delay input and the other signal line to Channel 1 of the mixer. Next, split the output of the effect patched into the feedback loop; send one signal line to the feedback loop receive jack, and the other signal line to Channel 2 of the mixer. With this patch you will not be using the delay's output mix control. Instead, mixer Channel 1 sets the straight signal level and mixer Channel 2 sets the delayed signal level. Since the echo output is being picked up after the processor, all echoes (including the first one) will be processed.

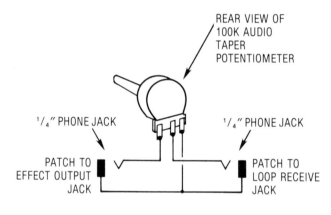

Figure 5-1

30 FOOT-CONTROLLED ECHO REPEAT

+ Volume pedal.

Background

With echo patches, turning up the front panel feedback control increases the number of echo repeats (see Application 13). However, for hands-free (or remote) operation, you may footpedal-control the amount of feedback—hence the number of repeats—if your delay includes feedback loop jacks.

Note: This application will not work with synthesizer control voltage pedals. You must use a standard volume pedal.

The Patch

Use standard patch C; patch the footpedal into the loop jacks as indicated.

Control Settings

Select the same settings as for a typical echo patch (see Application 13), but rather than using the front panel feedback control, push down on the footpedal to increase the number of repeats and pull back on the pedal to decrease the number of repeats.

Feedback (Regeneration). If the feedback control sets the overall level of the signal going through the loop jacks (example 2 at the beginning of this chapter), before inserting the footpedal in the feedback path loop set feedback for the maximum desired number of repeats. This helps tailor the footpedal range to your specific application.

31 VOCAL SIBILANCE ECHO

+ Outboard equalizer (parametric, graphic, and so on).

Background

See Application 26, then note that this application differs in two ways: first, using the feedback loop jacks eliminates the need for a stereo mixer; and, second, each echo becomes progressively brighter (unlike Application 26, where all echoes have the same timbre).

The Patch

See standard patch C; patch the equalizer into the loop jacks as indicated.

Control Settings

Set the controls as you would for standard echo (Application 13), then thin out the echo sound by adjusting the equalizer for a treble boost, bass cut, or both (whatever works best). You may need to re-adjust the feedback and input controls as you change the equalizer settings. As with Application 26, remember that boosting the treble is more likely to overload the delay line than cutting the bass.

Also try reversing the feedback phase (if possible), since one position will probably sound better than the other.

Tweaking the Patch

Experiment with various equalizer settings to see what sounds best with a particular voice.

32 PERCUSSIVE (CHOPPED) ECHO

+ Outboard noise gate.

Background

Noise gates can make signals more percussive by cutting off long decays. Similarly, they can cut off the decay of signals going through the delay line's feedback loop to create percussive echoes. This patch is particularly effective with the guitar, bass, drums, piano, and similar percussive instruments.

The Patch

See standard patch C; patch the noise gate into the loop jacks as indicated.

Control Settings

Use the same settings recommended for a typical echo patch (see Application 13). The only difference between this patch and other echo patches is the way in which the echoes are processed. Initially set the noise gate for medium sensitivity (also called *threshold*) and maximum noise reduction.

Tweaking the Patch

The higher the noise gate threshold, the more percussive the sound. Lowering the threshold will restore a natural sound.

You can also set the threshold so that the dynamics of your playing gate the echo feedback. By playing softly (i.e., below the threshold), the noise gate will be closed and no feedback will reach the delay input. If you play more forcefully and exceed the threshold, the noise gate will let the feedback signal through, thus enabling the echo effect.

33 ECHO PLUS REVERB EFFECTS

+ Outboard reverb unit.

Background

By patching a reverb unit into the delay's feedback path loop jacks, and setting the feedback control for multiple echoes, each successive echo will not only diminish in volume but also become increasingly reverberated. This provides a novel ambience effect.

The Patch

See standard patch C; patch the reverb into the loop jacks as indicated.

Control Settings

Use the same settings recommended for a typical echo patch (see Application 13). The only difference between this patch and other echo patches is the way in which the echoes are processed.

Tweaking the Patch

Be conservative with the reverb unit settings, since adding too much reverb will create a murky sound. A reverb unit with a blend (mix) control allows for feeding back some straight signal as well as the reverberated signal, thus providing a clear echo sound as well as the reverberated echoes.

34 PITCH CHANGED ECHO

+ Pitch transposer, harmony synthesizer, or *Harmonizer* (trademark of Eventide Clockworks).

Background

Patching a pitch transposer into the feedback loop lets successive echoes either rise or fall in pitch. Example: With the pitch transposer set to transpose up a major third, the first time an echo passes through the feedback path it will be transposed up a major third; the second time it passes through the loop it will be transposed up another major third; and so on until reaching the upper response limit of the pitch transposition device. (this may not sound too exciting on paper, but just wait until you check it out . . .)

The Patch

See standard patch C, and patch the pitch transposer into the loop jacks as indicated.

Control Settings

Use the same settings recommended for a typical echo patch (see Application 13). The only difference between this patch and other echo patches is the way in which the echoes are processed.
Pitch Transposer Controls. Initially select 100 percent transposed sound (no straight signal), then set the transposition amount. For this patch, use minimum pitch transposer feedback.

Tweaking the Patch

This is a fairly critical patch to get just right, since pitch transposers have various limitations (limited range, poor frequency response, and so on) and these greatly influence the overall sound. Experiment to find the best settings.

35 CHROMATIC GLISSANDO

+ Pitch transposer, harmony synthesizer, or *Harmonizer* (trademark of Eventide Clockworks).

Background

This application takes any sound played through the delay and synthesizes an upward or downward chromatic glissando from that sound.

The Patch

See standard patch C; patch the pitch transposer into the loop jacks as indicated.

Control Settings

While this patch is similar to previous echo applications (such as Application 13), set the delay line's feedback control at minimum so that the sound makes only one pass through the pitch transposer.
Pitch Transposer Controls. Select an output mix of 100 percent transposed sound, and transpose either plus or minus a half step (depending on whether you want an upward or downward gliss respectively). Initially turn the pitch transposer's feedback control up halfway.

Tweaking the Patch

The pitch transposer control settings are quite important: too much transposer feedback will clutter the sound, while too little feedback will cut the gliss short. Tweak the controls until you find a good compromise setting.

36 SHORTWAVE RECEIVER SOUND EFFECTS

+ Signal generator or synthesizer capable of high audio frequency operation.

Background

Intentionally feeding very high frequency signals into a delay line can cause interference between the input signal and the delay line's internal circuitry. This *aliasing* effect typically produces random, strange sounds at the delay line audio output that sound somewhat like tuning across a short wave band. This patch may not work with high quality delay lines that include extensive input filtering to keep out excessively high frequency signals; however, less expensive devices usually work quite well for this admittedly bizarre application.

The Patch

Plug a signal generator or synthesizer into the delay line loop receive jack, and listen to the output (see **Figure 5-2**). In some cases, plugging into the delay's input jack will produce better results; try both options and see which you prefer.

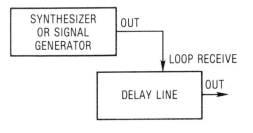

Figure 5-2

Control Settings

Initial Delay. If the delay line includes a fine delay control, set initial delay around 100 to 200 ms. If there is no fine delay control, set the delay time selector to a long delay (greater than 200 ms).

Fine Delay. Initially set fine delay for maximum delay, which lowers the delay line's clock frequency and makes it easier to create aliasing. *Feedback (Regeneration), Feedback Phase, Modulation Width, Modulation Speed.* These controls are the key to getting some extremely weird sounds, so play around with them once you get the basic patch working. It's impossible to be more specific as this patch is quite abstract.

Output Mix. Set for 100 percent delayed sound.

Tweaking the Patch

If you are playing a synthesizer, use a waveform with lots of harmonics (square or sawtooth wave), turn the synthesizer filter (VCF) up to its highest possible cutoff frequency, and turn up the output as high as possible. If this doesn't produce aliasing, play on the keyboard's top octave, increase the delay time, or increase the delay line input sensitivity. Play different notes and vary the initial delay to produce different effects.

If you are feeding the delay line with a signal generator, simply increase the signal generator's frequency and output level until you obtain aliasing.

If none of your efforts produce weird sounds, congratulations: you have a high-quality delay line with excellent input filtering. Unfortunately, you will not be able to abuse this kind of delay for the desired results.

37 RUNAWAY ECHOES

+ Outboard preamp.

Background

One of the most popular sound effects in early sci-fi and horror movies was to turn up a tape echo unit's feedback control so high that the echoes turned into a continuous, oscillating sound. However, this effect is difficult to obtain with modern delay lines; runaway feedback is generally considered undesirable, so most delays intentionally limit the maximum possible amount of feedback. Fortunately, inserting a preamp into a delay line's feedback loop jacks can circumvent the good intentions of design engineers and re-create a classic 1950s sound effect.

The Patch

See standard patch C. There is usually no need to plug anything into the input unless you can't get the runaway feedback process started.

Control Settings

Initial Delay. Start off with a delay time somewhere in the 100 to 200 ms range.
Fine Delay. Initially set at midpoint.
Feedback (Regeneration). Initially select maximum feedback.
Feedback Phase. Select positive feedback.
Modulation Width. Set for minimum modulation.
Modulation Speed. It does not matter with minimum modulation.
Output Mix. Set for 100 percent delayed sound.

Tweaking the Patch

Increase the preamp gain until you hear a continuous series of runaway echoes; if the sound becomes too ugly and distorted, turn down the feedback control. If desired, fool with the modulation controls to alter the basic sound.

38 MIXING TWO SIGNALS INTO A DELAY LINE

Background

Need a two input mixer in an emergency? While this patch doesn't use much of the delay line's capabilities (and there certainly are simpler ways to mix two signals together), most delay lines with feedback path loop jacks can mix two signals together.

The Patch

Refer to **Figure 5–3**, which shows how to connect two signals into the delay line.

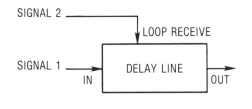

Figure 5–3

Control Settings

It is difficult to recommend exact settings due to design differences between delay lines. With most delays, the signal plugged into the loop receive jack will travel through the delay line along with the input signal. In this case, select minimum delay, no modulation, and set output mix for 100 percent delayed sound. Varying feedback will usually regulate the level of the signal plugged into the loop receive jack. If the feedback control has no effect, varying the output mix control may affect the blend of the two sounds.

Chapter 6

Drum Delay Line Applications

39 TUNING PERCUSSIVE SOUNDS

Background

Delay lines can give a sense of pitch to unpitched sounds (white noise, cymbals, handclaps, and so on), thus helping to tune drum and percussion tracks to a specific key.

Control Settings

Control settings are similar to Application 6 (comb filtering).
Initial Delay. Select an initial delay time between 0 and 10 ms.
Fine Delay. Initially turn up halfway.
Feedback (Regeneration). Turn up as high as possible short of runaway feedback.
Feedback Phase. Positive feedback gives you the strongest sense of pitch.
Modulation Width. Select minimum modulation.
Modulation Speed. It does not matter with minimum modulation.
Output Mix. Initially set for 100 percent delayed sound.

Tweaking the Patch

With maximum feedback there should be a strong sense of pitch. Fine delay varies the tuning, while feedback phase varies the timbre.

To make the effect less obvious, decrease feedback or set the output mix for more straight signal.

40 AUTOMATIC TOM FLAMMER

+ Mixer, drum machine with individual tom outputs.

Background

A drum *flam* occurs when a drummer strikes the same drum twice in quick succession. This sound resembles slapback echo, and is often applied to toms.

The Patch

To flam the toms without flamming the other drums, plug the toms into a mixer, assign them to a separate submix, send the submix out into the delay, and bring the delay output back into the mixer (see **Figure 6-1**). If your mixer does not allow for submixing, plug the individual tom outputs into a separate utility mixer, feed that mixer output into the delay input, then bring the delay output back into a channel of the main mixer (see **Figure 6-2**).

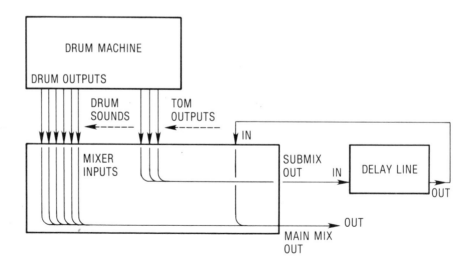

Figure 6-1

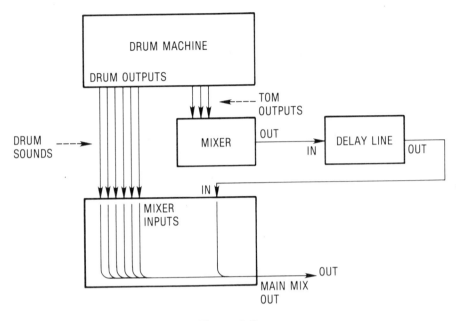

Figure 6–2

Control Settings

The settings are similar to slapback echo.

Initial Delay. Select a 25 to 50 ms flam repeat time.

Feedback (Regeneration). Select minimum feedback to hear a single flam instead of multiple echoes.

Feedback Phase. It does not matter with minimum feedback.

Modulation Width. Select minimum modulation.

Modulation Speed. It does not matter with minimum modulation.

Output Mix. Initially set for 50 percent straight and 50 percent delayed sound. Emphasize or de-emphasize the flam by selecting more or less delayed sound respectively.

Bypass Switch. Use to bring the flam effect in and out as desired.

Tweaking the Patch

Since delay time sets the time interval between the two drum sounds, it is the most important patch parameter and should ideally relate to the tempo of the music (see Application 16).

41 DRUM MACHINE HANDCLAP REALISM ENHANCER

+ Mixer, drum machine with individual sound outputs.

Background

Unlike humans, drum machines make exactly the same handclap sound every time—which is not always desirable. Processing the drum machine handclaps with a tight, slightly modulated echo creates a more randomized handclap effect that sounds more human. Depending on how the modulation affects the echo time at any given moment, the delayed handclaps can occur further apart from, or closer to, the straight handclaps. Modulation also adds some pitch-shifting that subtly changes the handclaps' timbre.

The Patch

Referring to **Figure 6–3**, patch the drum machine's handclap output into the delay line input. Patch the other drum sounds, and the delay line output, into the mixer. Bring up the appropriate channels for the desired drum sound mix.

Control Settings

This is basically slapback echo with added modulation.
Initial Delay. Typically 20 ms, but try anywhere from 10 to 40 ms.
Feedback (Regeneration). Initially select minimum feedback.
Feedback Phase. It does not matter with minimum feedback.
Modulation Width. Turn up as much as possible, short of obtaining an out-of-tune sound.
Modulation Speed. Set for a moderate speed (say, 4 Hz).
Output Mix. Initially select 50 percent straight and 50 percent delayed sounds. For a subtler effect, reduce the delayed signal.

Tweaking the Patch

The crucial controls are initial delay, modulation width, and modulation speed. The more you increase modulation, the more radical the timing variations between the delayed and straight handclaps. Optimum delay time is a matter of taste, but tight delays seem to work best. Adding feedback sparingly might also be indicated for some applications.

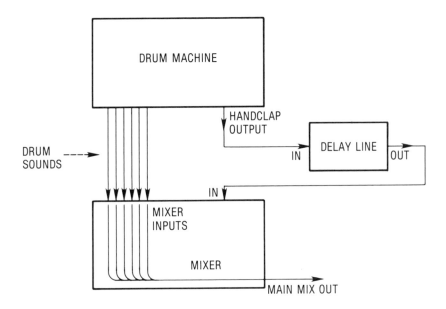

Figure 6-3

42 EXTENDING ELECTRONIC DRUM CYMBAL DECAY

+ Mixer, drum machine with individual cymbal output.

Background

Storing long-decay drum sounds (such as cymbals) in digital drums requires a lot of computer memory. To conserve memory, and therefore cost, most companies shorten these sounds by truncating their decays. A delay line can artificially extend an electronic cymbal's decay for a more natural sound.

The Patch

Same as **Figure 6–3**, except plug the cymbal output (instead of the indicated handclap output) into the delay line.

Control Settings

The object is to add some very tight, almost reverb-like echoes with a fair amount of feedback.
Initial Delay. Set for 23–25 ms.
Feedback (Regeneration). Initially add about 50 percent feedback.
Feedback Phase. Select positive feedback for the most metallic sound. This seems to go well with cymbals.
Modulation Width. Select minimum modulation.
Modulation Speed. It does not matter with minimum modulation.
Output Mix. Set for about 65 percent straight and 35 percent delayed sound.

Tweaking the Patch

Increase feedback to lengthen the cymbal's decay; use output mix to set the synthesized decay level. Note that the delay must be short enough so that you do not hear individual echoes, but rather, a stream of sound.

If the delay includes a feedback path loop (see Chapter 5), try inserting an equalizer (see Application 14) into the loop to change the timbre of the decay. Decreasing the treble will give a progressively more muted decay, while increasing the treble will give a progressively brighter decay.

43 *I-LIKE-THAT-HI-HAT* HI-HAT PROCESSOR

Background

This application was suggested by Craig O'Donnell (of the group *Scientific Americans*), who discovered it while trying to make an uninteresting hi-hat sound interesting. The patch produces a rough, industrial-noise hi-hat by jamming as much signal as possible into the delay and then adding some modulation. Craig recommends using this effect with DeltaLab's *Effectron* series, because he feels that these units overload in a more pleasing way than the other delay lines he has tried.

Control Settings

Unlike all the other applications in this book, turn up the input control so that the overload LED is *on* as much as possible.

Initial Delay. Select a short to medium delay (whichever sounds best in the mix).

Fine Delay. Adjust later to change tonality.

Feedback (Regeneration). Adjust to suit yourself; start off with minimum feedback.

Feedback Phase. It doesn't matter with minimum feedback.

Modulation Width. Turn up modulation about 33 percent.

Modulation Speed. Select a slow modulation speed.

Output Mix. Initially set for 50 percent straight and 50 percent delayed sound.

Tweaking the Patch

When listening to the delayed sound only, a short delay (under 10 ms) will prevent the hi-hat sound from lagging behind the beat. When listening to a mix of straight and delayed sounds, try to synchronize the echo time to the tempo of the song, especially with longer echoes (see Application 16).

Varying the input level control for different amounts of distortion provides different timbres; the more level, the grittier the sound.

44 DRIVING ELECTRONIC DRUMS FROM A DELAY LINE WITH A CLOCK (SYNC) OUTPUT

+ Delay line clock (sync) output feature for driving electronic drums, electronic drums compatible with the delay line clock signal.

Background

Most electronic drum units have *external clock input* jacks. These allow the drums to be driven by an external synchronizing clock instead of the drum's internal clock generator. DeltaLab, Lexicon, and Roland all manufacture delay lines that send out suitable clock signals. The delay's clock frequency (which sets the drum's tempo) varies with the delay time; typically, the delay time equals one or two measures of music played on the electronic drums. Since the echo time is always synchronized to the drum tempo, the echo sound is more rhythmically appropriate.

Note, however, that not all drum machines accept the same standard clock signal. The MXR Drum Computer accepts a 24-pulses-per-quarter-note clock, the LinnDrum 48-pulses-per-quarter-note, the Oberheim DMX 96-pulses-per-quarter-note, and the E-mu Drumulator can accept any of the above. Therefore, check that your particular drum unit is compatible with your delay's clock signal. If the two don't match up, there is one consolation: Since 24, 48, and 96 are all multiples of each other, you can always program the drums in double-time or half-time to compensate. Example: If your drum machine accepts a 48-pulses-per-quarter-note clock, and the delay puts out a 24-pulses-per-quarter-note clock, program a double-time drum part. Feeding the drum with a half-speed clock signal will then give the desired tempo. Or, if your drum machine accepts a 24-pulses-per-quarter-note clock, and the delay puts out a 48-pulses-per-quarter-note clock, program a half-time drum part.

The Patch

Referring to **Figure 6-4**, patch the delay line clock output signal into the electronic drum external clock input. Patch the drum unit audio output (or any other audio output) into the delay.

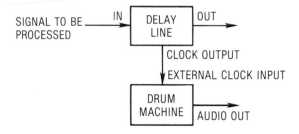

Figure 6-4

Control Settings

Since the clock speed ties in with the delay time, you will usually choose a long initial delay when driving electronic drums. (Note: If you switch to a short delay time range, some newer delays slow down the clock correspondingly. This makes the clock signal useful at shorter delays as well as longer delays.)

Initial Delay. Use this control to set tempo instead of the electronic drum machine's tempo control.

Feedback (Regeneration). Depending on the desired effect, turn up for multiple echoes or down for a single echo.

Feedback Phase. Positive feedback preferred.

Modulation Width. Generally keep modulation at minimum except for special effects.

Modulation Speed. It does not matter with minimum modulation.

Output Mix. Set for the desired blend of echo and straight sound for the signal being processed.

Tweaking the Patch

Setting the tempo usually locks you into a particular delay time. However, you can still introduce modulation or vary the feedback and output mix controls to alter the echo effect.

Chapter 7

Echotron *Applications*

Chapter Background

The *Echotron*, made by DeltaLab Research, was the first low-cost long (250 ms to 4 seconds) delay line. It treats the delay time as equivalent to one measure of music (see Application 16 to understand the relationship between musical rhythm and delay time), and provides a synchronized metronome output for playing along in sync with the echo time. There is also a synchronized clock pulse signal for driving electronic drums (see Application 44), synchronized infinite repeat (i.e., infinite repeat always starts and ends on the beat), as well as standard delay line features such as feedback and feedback path tone control (see Application 14). Although the *Echotron* clock output is normally 48-pulses-per-quarter-note, it can be changed to 24- or 96-pulses-per-quarter-note if either one is more appropriate for your equipment (see Application 50).

While these applications pertain specifically to the *Echotron*, many of them should be useable with other delays that include similar features. Also note that the long delay applications mentioned earlier (13, 14, 19, 20, 24, 25, 28, and so on) are well-suited to the *Echotron*.

The *Echotron* has a range switch that selects between two ranges, 250–1,024 ms and 1,024–4,096 ms. All the applications in this chapter assume the longer range setting; however, the shorter delay range can also be useful. With this range selected, the delay time equals a quarter note (of a measure played on the drums).

Note: The *Echotron* refers to the output mix control as the delay mix control, and so will we in this chapter.

45 SYNCHRONIZING SYNTHESIZER ARPEGGIATOR TO QUARTER NOTES

+ Synthesizer with external arpeggiator clock input jack.

Background

Many synthesizers include automatic arpeggiators to play sequentially any notes being held down. A front panel control usually sets the tempo, however, some synthesizers also include an *external clock input* jack on the back for external arpeggiator tempo control. Plugging a compatible synchronization signal into this jack overrides the internal tempo control and drives the synthesizer arpeggiator from the external clock.

The *Echotron*'s metronome signal provides one pulse per quarter note. Therefore, patching this signal to the synthesizer's external clock input will trigger the arpeggiator on every quarter note. (Incidentally, processing the synth through the *Echotron* works well since the delay time and arpeggiator rate are precisely synchronized.)

The Patch

In **Figure 7-1**, the *Echotron* metronome output plugs into the synthesizer's external clock input. The signal to be processed plugs into the Echotron's audio input.

Control Settings

The synthesizer arpeggiator rate is affected solely by the Echotron delay time (since the delay time controls the metronome output rate). Set the remaining controls for the desired effect—echo (Application 13), solid-state loop effects (Application 24), digital recording (Application 25), and so on.

Initial Delay. Select the *Echotron*'s 4096 ms range, and adjust the delay control for the desired arpeggiator rate.

Feedback, Modulation, Delay Mix Control, and so on. Adjust to suit yourself.

Tweaking the Patch

To trigger the arpeggiator every eighth note, cut the delay time in half and if you are driving a drum unit from the *Echotron* sync (clock) output, program the drums in half-time.

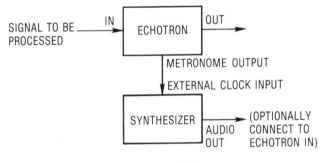

Figure 7-1

46 SYNCHRONIZING SYNTHESIZER ARPEGGIATOR TO VARIOUS NOTE VALUES

+ Synthesizer with external arpeggiator clock input jack, electronic drum machine with programmable metronome output *and* 24-, 48-, or 96-pulses-per-quarter-note external clock input.

Background

The previous application limits the synthesizer arpeggiator rate to quarter-note or eighth-note rhythms. However, if your drum unit includes a programmable metronome output and is synched to the *Echotron* (see Application 44), the arpeggiator can be triggered from the drum metronome output (which will be synched to the *Echotron*) at any of the drum machine's available metronome rates. (Note: You do not need to listen to the drum's audio output if you want to hear only the synthesizer sound; the drums can be treated strictly as an interfacing/synchronizing device.)

The Patch

Referring to **Figure 7–2**, the *Echotron* sync (clock) output plugs into the drum machine's 48-pulses-per-quarter-note external clock input (see Application 50 if your drums require a 24- or 96-pulses-per-quarter-note clock signal), and the drum machine's metronome output plugs into the synthesizer's external clock input. The signal to be processed plugs into the *Echotron*'s audio input.

Control Settings

The synthesizer arpeggiator rate is affected by the drum's programmed metronome setting and by the *Echotron* delay time (since the delay time controls the drum tempo, which in turn controls the metronome output). Set the remaining controls for the desired effect—echo

(Application 13), solid-state loop effects (Application 24), digital recording (Application 25), and so on.

Initial Delay. Select the *Echotron*'s 4096 ms range, and set the delay control and drum unit metronome for the desired arpeggiator rate.

Feedback, Modulation, Delay Mix Control, and so on. Adjust to suit yourself.

Tweaking the Patch

To trigger two synthesizers at different rates, trigger one synthesizer from the drum machine's programmable metronome at one rate, and another synthesizer directly from the *Echotron* metronome output at another rate.

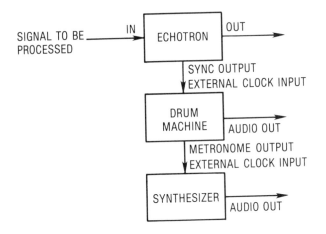

Figure 7-2

47 FLANGED DRUMS

+ Electronic drum machine with 24-, 48-, or 96-pulses-per-quarter-note external clock input.

Background

While the *Echotron* normally cannot provide flanging, some limited flanging effects are possible if you drive the drum clock input from the *Echotron*'s sync output. This flanging is true through-zero flanging (see Applications 60 and 61) and has a pseudo-randomized flange sweep.

The Patch

See **Figure 7-3**. Feed the *Echotron*'s sync output into the drum machine's external clock input (see Application 50 if your drums require a 24- or 96-pulses-per-quarter-note clock signal). Send the drum's audio output to the *Echotron* input, then send the *Echotron* output to your monitor amp.

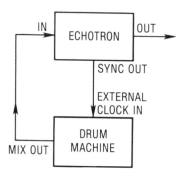

Figure 7-3

Control Settings

This patch works only under very specific conditions. The length of the drum pattern to be flanged must equal the echo time (as set by the delay control in the *Echotron*'s 4096 ms range), and must repeat more than once.

To best hear the flanging effect, program a repetitive drum pattern that uses lots of cymbal sounds. As the drums play, the first time the pattern cycles through you will not hear flanging. However, flanging will occur on all subsequent passes of that same pattern.

Feedback. Turn up about 66 percent.

Delay Mix Control. Set for 50 percent straight and 50 percent delayed sound.

Tweaking the Patch

This patch works because the *Echotron* delay time drifts very slightly—not enough to notice but enough to create flanging.

The first time a pattern plays, it is also being loaded into the *Echotron*'s memory. When you hear the drum pattern for the second time, you also hear the original sound being read out of memory at almost—but not quite—the same time. Mixing these two virtually identical signals together produces the flanging effect.

Because the *Echotron* clock does not drift very much, the flanging may not vary too much from the through-zero position. If this causes too thin a sound, either select more straight sound with the delay mix control or vary the delay time control very slightly. (Varying this control will alter the tempo; however, the amount of variation needed to beef up the flanging sound is much smaller than the amount of variation required to make a noticeable tempo difference.)

Turning feedback up adds more overdubs, which intensify (and further randomize) the flanging effect. Turning feedback down gives a crisper flanging effect.

48 FLANGED DRUMS WITH PSYCHO-ACOUSTIC PANNING

+ Electronic drum machine, stereo mixer.

Background

This resembles Application 47 and shares the same limitations (i.e., the drum pattern length must equal the echo time as set by the delay control while in the 4096 ms range, and you will not hear flanging on the first pass of the drums but on all subsequent passes of that same pattern). However, setting this patch up in stereo allows for some unusual psycho-acoustic stereo panning effects instead of a typical flanging sound. (If you pan the stereo outputs to mono, you will hear flanging instead of panning.) These effects are particularly dramatic when monitored on headphones.

The Patch

Feed the *Echotron*'s clock output into the drum machine's external clock input (see Application 50 if your drums require a 24- or 96-pulses-per-quarter-note clock signal). Referring to **Figure 7–4**, send the drum's audio output simultaneously to the *Echotron* input and one channel of a stereo mixer. Send the *Echotron* output to the other mixer channel. Pan the two mixer channels left and right.

Control Settings

The control settings are similar to those in Application 47, but set delay mix for 100 percent delayed sound to create a good stereo image.
Initial Delay. Use the *Echotron*'s 4096 ms range, and adjust delay for the desired drum machine tempo.
Feedback. Turn up about 66 percent.
Delay Mix Control. Set for 100 percent delayed sound.

Tweaking the Patch

To make the panning effect more complex and somewhat more randomized, turn up the feedback control.

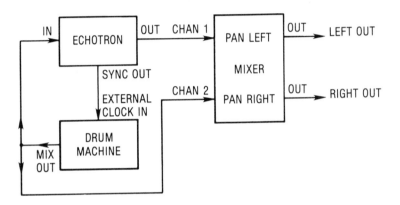

Figure 7-4

49 TWO-MEASURE *ECHOTRON* ECHO

+ Any drum machine that can accept a 24-pulses-per-quarter-note external clock signal.

Background

Normally, the *Echotron* delay time equals one measure of music played on a drum machine. However, by feeding the *Echotron*'s 48-pulses-per-quarter-note signal into a drum unit that accepts a 24-pulses-per-quarter note signal, the *Echotron* delay time will equal two measures of music played on the drum machine. You will need to set the *Echotron* for twice as much delay as you would normally select for a regular, single-measure echo.

The Patch

See **Figure 7–5**. Patch the *Echotron*'s sync signal into the drum machine external clock input.

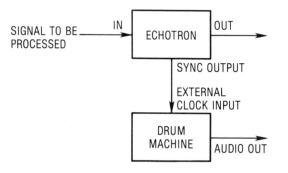

Figure 7–5

Control Settings

Initial Delay. Select the *Echotron*'s 4096 ms range and adjust initial delay for the desired tempo. Due to the 2:1 clock mismatch between the drums and *Echotron*, the delay time will now equal two measures.
Feedback. Initially select minimum feedback.
Delay Mix. Adjust for the desired mix of straight and delayed sounds.

Tweaking the Patch

Adding more feedback gives a denser sound, although most times you will probably prefer the effect of no feedback.

50 ALTERING THE *ECHOTRON* SYNC OUTPUT SIGNAL

Background

As mentioned earlier, most drum units accept either a 24-, 48-, or 96-pulses-per-quarter-note external clock signal. While the *Echotron* clock normally sends out 48-pulses-per-quarter-note, a simple hardware modification selects one of the other two sync pulse standards. Note that the factory will not perform this modification, and that attempting to do this modification yourself will void the warranty—so do it carefully!

Making the Modification

This mod requires re-wiring a jumper inside the unit. Take off the *Echotron*'s top cover, then locate the three circuit board jumpers labelled I, J, and K in the vicinity of the output jack. Break the solder link between the two J pads with a sharp knife. Add a solder link between the two I pads for a 24-pulses-per-quarter-note sync pulse, or between the two K pads for a 96-pulses-per-quarter-note sync pulse.

Chapter 8

Using the Control Voltage Input

Chapter Background

Many digital delays include a *control voltage input* jack to allow for external delay time control. Feeding a low-level DC voltage (typically 0 to +5V, but sometimes 0 to +10V) into this jack varies the delay; lesser voltages usually give longer delays and higher voltages shorter delays. The applications in this chapter all assume that the delay line has a delay time control voltage input.

Suitable Control Voltage Generators

A control voltage (CV for short) input needs to be driven by a *control voltage output*. Many keyboard synthesizers, and some special effects, generate suitable CV outputs. Example: Most analog synthesizers include a *keyboard CV output* whose voltage increases as you play higher up on the keyboard (see Application 56). Some synthesizers also provide a CV output from the LFO (modulation source). This provides cyclic, low frequency waveforms that can automatically sweep the delay time.

Another control voltage source, the *control voltage pedal*, resembles a standard footpedal but instead of controlling volume, it generates a variable CV output. Pushing down on the pedal increases the CV output, while pulling back on the pedal decreases the CV output. Application 51 describes how to convert a standard volume pedal into a control voltage pedal.

Finally, modular synthesizers provide a wealth of control voltage outputs that can help create truly innovative effects.

Important

Depending on your particular delay line, plugging into the CV input can affect the action of the front panel fine delay control (if present) in one of three ways:

1. The fine delay control will become inoperative (the CV input overrides fine delay).

2. The fine delay control acts as an attenuator for the signal plugged into the CV input. Example: If the CV output varies the delay line over too wide a range, turning down fine delay will reduce the control voltage's effect.

3. The fine delay control will be independent of the CV input. Therefore, fine delay will set the initial delay, and the CV input will add to the fine delay setting.

Consult the owner's manual, or try one of the applications in this chapter, to determine how your delay line reacts. If it is (1), simply ignore the fine delay control when using the control voltage input. If it is (2), initially turn fine delay to the *shortest* delay (which should allow for maximum control voltage sweep; if not, set for the *longest* delay instead) and trim later if necessary. If it is (3), initially turn fine delay to the longest delay and leave it there so that as you experiment, the delay line reacts only to the CV input.

Note that if your delay line acts as described in (1) or (3), the CV will always sweep the delay over the widest possible range. For subtler effects, add an external *attenuator* (level control) between the CV output and the delay line's control voltage input (see **Figure 8-1**) so that you can regulate the amount of control voltage being injected into the delay line.

Incidentally, some delays treat the external control voltage input as part of the modulation section. Therefore, the modulation width control might be disabled if you plug into the CV input, or it might act as an attenuator for the signal plugged into the CV input. In the case of the former, you may have to insert an attenuator (as described below; see **Figure 8-1**) between the CV output and the delay's CV input. In the case of the latter, leave modulation width up full when plugged into the CV input, and trim if necessary.

Confused? I'm not surprised! The only way to understand all this is to practice, and listen to how different controls react when you're using the CV input. After a while (and possibly some frustration), you'll get to know your delay line well enough to use the CV input to good advantage.

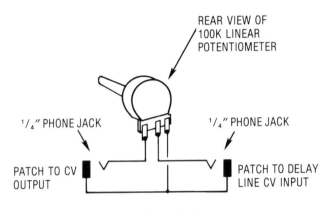

Figure 8–1

51 VOLUME PEDAL TO CONTROL VOLTAGE PEDAL CONVERSION

Background

A control voltage pedal provides a variable control voltage output suitable for driving a delay line's CV input. Pushing down on the pedal *increases* the CV output, while pulling back on the pedal *decreases* the CV output.

Converting a Volume Pedal into a Control Voltage Pedal

You must use a standard, passive volume pedal for this conversion. If the pedal uses batteries or requires AC power, it is not suitable.

Solder a 9V transistor radio battery connector to a ¼″ phone plug as shown in **Figure 8–2**. Note that the connector's red lead goes to the plug's hot terminal, while the connector's black lead goes to the plug's ground terminal. Plug this plug into the pedal's input jack, then patch the pedal's output jack to the delay line's CV input jack. Clip a battery to the battery connector, and vary the pedal position to vary the CV output between 0 and +9 volts.

BATTERY
CONNECTOR

¼″ PHONE
PLUG

Figure 8–2

52 PEDAL FLANGING

+ Control voltage footpedal (see Application 51).

Background

Pedal flanging provides foot control of the flanging sweep. Unlike automatic flanging (Application 2), the sweep rate can be roughly synchronized to the music by how you rock the footpedal. As with previously mentioned flanging applications, delay lines with a wide sweep range give the most dramatic flanging effect.

The Patch

See standard patch D. The pedal's CV output feeds the delay line's CV input.

Control Settings

Control settings are similar to those for manual flanging (Application 1).

Initial Delay. With the pedal pushed all the way down, set initial delay for the top of the sweep (the shortest delay you will want). Pulling back on the pedal should lengthen the delay time.

Fine Delay. Refer to *Important* at the beginning of this chapter.

Feedback (Regeneration), Feedback Phase. See manual flanging (Application 1).

Modulation Width. Select minimum modulation. If plugging in and varying a control voltage in later steps doesn't create a sweep, then turn modulation width up all the way and refer to *Important* at the beginning of this chapter.

Modulation Speed. It does not matter with minimum modulation.

Output Mix. Set for 50 percent straight and 50 percent delayed sound.

Tweaking the Patch

Varying the footpedal position varies the flange sweep. Work the footpedal in such a way that the flanger sweep goes well with the music.

53 PEDAL PITCH-BENDING

+ Control voltage footpedal (see Application 51).

Background

At medium and long delay settings, sweeping the delay time with a footpedal creates pitch-bending effects. (Also see Application 22.)

The Patch

See standard patch D. The pedal CV output feeds the delay line CV input.

Control Settings

Control settings are similar to those used for medium-length echoes.
Initial Delay. Select an initial delay in the 50 to 100 ms range.
Fine Delay. The setting of this control is not particularly critical; tweak it up later on (also refer to *Important* at the beginning of this chapter).
Feedback (Regeneration). Initially select minimum feedback.
Feedback Phase. It doesn't matter with minimum feedback.
Modulation Width. Select minimum modulation. If plugging in and varying a control voltage in later steps doesn't create a sweep, then turn modulation width up all the way and refer to *Important* at the beginning of this chapter.
Modulation Speed. It does not matter with minimum modulation.
Output Mix. Initially set for 50 percent straight and 50 percent delayed sound.

Tweaking the Patch

Vary the footpedal position to bend pitch; the amount of pitch bend will increase at longer delays. For more unusual effects, add some feedback. To hear the pitch-bended sound by itself, set output mix to 100 percent delayed sound.

54 PITCH-SHIFTED DRUMS

+ Drum unit with clock output.

Background

This application, suggested by Kevin Monahan of E-mu Systems, provides a strangely pitch-shifted drum sound. It works by switching the delay time between the high and low end of a delay range at a very fast rate, thus providing a primitive harmonization effect.

The Patch

See **Figure 8-3**. If your drum unit does not have a clock out, try using its metronome (click) output set for a fast rate (i.e., thirty-second note triplets or sixty-fourth notes).

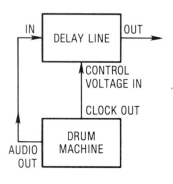

Figure 8-3

Control Settings

You're pretty much on your own—the exact effect will depend upon the drum tempo, drum clock output waveform, delay line sweep range, initial delay setting, and other factors.

Initial Delay. Longer delays give more extreme sounds. Start off with about 25 ms.

Fine Delay. Refer to *Important* at the beginning of this chapter.

Feedback (Regeneration). Start off at minimum. Increase for weird effects.

Feedback Phase. Positive feedback preferred.

Modulation Width. Select minimum modulation. If plugging in the drum's clock output doesn't create any tonal change, then turn modulation width up all the way and refer to *Important* at the beginning of this chapter.

Modulation Speed. It does not matter with minimum modulation.

Output Mix. Initially set for 50 percent straight and 50 percent delayed sound.

Tweaking the Patch

Delay time is the most influential control, although adjusting feedback will also alter the sound. This patch works best with wide sweep range delay lines.

55 PITCH TRANSPOSING

+ Sawtooth wave CV generator (as found on some synthesizers).

Background

Delay lines can transpose pitch over a limited range, although with far less fidelity than devices optimized for pitch transposition (i.e., *MXR Pitch Transposer, Eventide Harmonizer*). Feeding a positive-going, low frequency sawtooth wave into the CV input transposes pitch upward; a negative-going sawtooth transposes pitch downwards. The overall sound will be glitchy and rough but can be useful for special effects. The greater the delay line sweep range, the greater the potential amount of transposition.

The Patch

See standard patch D. The sawtooth CV generator feeds the delay time CV input.

Control Settings

Control settings are quite crucial and will require a lot of tweaking for optimum results.

Initial Delay. Select a delay time in the chorus/doubling range (25 ms or so).

Fine Delay. If the patch doesn't seem to work, refer to *Important* at the beginning of this chapter and experiment with the Fine Delay control.

Feedback (Regeneration). Select minimum feedback.

Feedback Phase. It doesn't matter with minimum feedback.

Modulation Width. Select minimum modulation. If plugging in and varying a control voltage in later steps doesn't create a sweep, then turn modulation width up all the way and refer to *Important* at the beginning of this chapter.

Modulation Speed. It does not matter with minimum modulation.

Output Mix. Initially set for 50 percent straight and 50 percent delayed sound.

Tweaking the Patch

The rate of the sawtooth control voltage generator, along with the initial delay time, determine the amount of transposition; experiment with both to achieve the most glitch-free transposition effect. Since the quality of the transposed sound will not be all that great, you might want to adjust the output mix control to place the transposed sound pretty much in the background.

56 KEYBOARD-CONTROLLED DELAY TIME

+ Synthesizer with keyboard CV output.

Background

Feeding the synthesizer's keyboard CV output into the delay time CV input lets you vary delay time from the keyboard. Don't expect a close correlation between delay time and keyboard pitch; in other words, playing an octave higher on the keyboard will not necessarily cut the delay time in half.

The Patch

See standard patch D. The keyboard CV output feeds the delay line's delay time CV input.

Control Settings

Control settings depend mostly on your intended application. When set for echo, the keyboard selects different echo times. When set for flanging, the keyboard controls the flange sweep.

Initial Delay, Fine Delay, Feedback (Regeneration), Feedback Phase, Output Mix. Adjust for the desired type of effect (flanging, echo, chorus, and so on) as described in previous applications.

Modulation Width. Select minimum modulation. If plugging in and varying a control voltage in later steps doesn't create a sweep, then turn modulation width up all the way and refer to *Important* at the beginning of this chapter.

Tweaking the Patch

To glide smoothly between delay times, add portamento to the keyboard. Vibrato, pitch bending, and other keyboard effects can also be useful.

57 RAINDROPS DELAY SOUND

+ Synthesizer with keyboard arpeggiator and CV output, *or* sample-and-hold CV generator.

Background

This application creates a tuned, semi-randomized tonality that abstractly resembles the sound of dripping water. It's quite pretty and particularly effective with guitar.

The Patch

See standard patch D. The keyboard CV output feeds the delay time CV input.

Control Settings

This effect works best with relatively short delay times.
Initial Delay. Select a short delay (flanging or chorusing range; approximately 12 ms).
Fine Delay. Generally this control is not too critical and may be tweaked up later to tune the patch (see *Tweaking the Patch*).
Feedback (Regeneration). Set for maximum possible feedback short of runaway feedback.
Feedback Phase. Initially select positive phase.
Modulation Width. Select minimun modulation. If plugging in and varying a control voltage in later steps doesn't create a sweep, then turn modulation width up all the way and refer to *Important* at the beginning of this chapter.
Modulation Speed. It does not matter with minimum modulation.
Output Mix. Initially adjust for 40 percent straight and 60 percent delayed sound. Adjust later to suit yourself.

Tweaking the Patch

Hold down a chord on the synthesizer and select arpeggiation. This feeds a series of discrete control voltages into the delay time CV input, causing the delay time to jump periodically between various values. For a more random effect, press keys randomly or use a sample-and-hold CV source instead of the arpeggiated keyboard.

This patch often imparts a strong sense of pitch to the signal being processed. Adjusting fine delay may help to tune the patch. As with the previous application, adding vibrato, pitch-bending, and so on, can further modify the sound.

58 APPLAUSE GENERATOR

+ Synthesizer with keyboard arpeggiator and CV output, *or* sample-and-hold CV generator.

Background

The reason why applause sounds complex is because each clap produces its own unique pitch and timbre. This application modifies the sound of one or two people clapping to create a more complex sound that resembles applause.

The Patch

See standard patch D. The keyboard CV output feeds the delay time CV input, while a microphone (to pick up the handclap sounds) feeds the delay line input.

Control Settings

This effect works best with delay times in the slapback/doubling range.
Initial Delay. Select a 30 to 100 ms delay.
Fine Delay. Generally the setting of this control is not too critical. However, if you encounter problems with this application refer to *Important* at the beginning of this chapter.
Feedback (Regeneration). Set for moderate-to-heavy amounts of feedback to provide multiple handclaps.
Feedback Phase. Select positive phase.
Modulation Width. Select minimum modulation. If plugging in and varying a control voltage in later steps doesn't create a sweep, then turn modulation width up all the way and refer to *Important* at the beginning of this chapter.
Modulation Speed. It does not matter with minimum modulation.
Output Mix. Initially adjust for about 60 percent delayed sound and 40 percent straight sound.

Tweaking the Patch

To test out the patch, have someone clap into the microphone. Hold down a fairly complex chord over a limited range of the synthesizer keyboard, then select arpeggiation. Vary initial delay, feedback, and the notes being held on the keyboard to obtain the desired effect. Adding slow keyboard vibrato (or slow modulation from the delay line controls) can also help randomize the applause sound.

59 AUTOMATIC PITCH-BEND FOR GUITAR

+ Envelope follower synthesizer module.

Background

This patch, while somewhat difficult to set up, provides automatic pitch-bending whenever you pluck a guitar string strongly.

The Patch

See **Figure 8-4**. The envelope follower can be a separate, stand-alone module or some synthesizers include a suitable internal audio input with envelope follower output. In either case, the envelope follower should provide a CV output proportional to the level of the guitar.

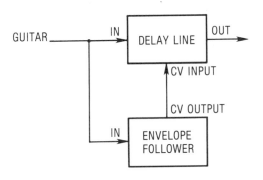

Figure 8-4

Control Settings

This effect seems to work best with delay times in the chorusing range.
Initial Delay. Select a relatively short delay (around 20 ms).
Fine Delay. The setting of this control is not particularly critical. However, if you encounter problems refer to *Important* at the beginning of this chapter.

Feedback (Regeneration).   Set for minimum feedback.

Feedback Phase. It does not matter with minimum feedback.

Modulation Width. Select minimum modulation. If plugging in (and playing through) the envelope follower doesn't create a sweep, then turn modulation width all the way up and refer to *Important* at the beginning of this chapter.

Modulation Speed. It does not matter with minimum modulation.

Output Mix. Select 100 percent delayed sound for the most realistic effect.

Tweaking the Patch

The greater the envelope follower output, the greater the amount of pitch-bend. Since the envelope follower's output is at its maximum during the guitar's attack, most of the pitch-bending will occur towards the beginning of a note. For less pitch-bending, decrease the delay time or insert an attenuator (as mentioned under *Important* in the beginning of this chapter) between the envelope follower CV output and delay time CV input. For more pronounced pitch bending, increase the delay time; however, this will produce a noticeable time lag between the time you play a note and the time you hear it.

Chapter 9

Multiple Delay Line Applications

Chapter Background

Using multiple delay lines opens up entirely new types of signal processing applications. While the following patches generally require more work to set up and adjust than previous patches, the results are well worth the extra effort.

Input Considerations

For most of the following applications, you will need to feed the signal to be processed into two delay line inputs simultaneously. Referring to **Figure 9-1**, patch the instrument output to a Y-cord or *multiple box* (several jacks wired in parallel), then run two cords to the delay inputs.

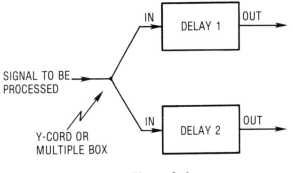

Figure 9-1

While most electronic instruments and tape outputs can drive multiple effect inputs, guitars and microphones usually cannot. If feeding an instrument to multiple delay line inputs produces a loading problem (resulting in a duller sound and less overall volume), insert a preamp, compressor, or other electronic effect between the instrument and the Y-cord (see **Figure 9-2**). These devices are all available commercially or may be built from plans in my first book, _Electronic Projects for Musicians_.

Output Considerations

For mono applications which simply mix the outputs together, a basic mono mixer and monitor will suffice. Companies such as Boss and Yamaha make suitable low-cost mixers (or you could build Project 18 from _Electronic Projects for Musicians_).

Stereo applications require a stereo mixer and stereo monitoring setup, as shown in standard patch E. A mixing console with two free inputs is perfect for multiple delay line applications. The console's _panpots_ let you pan the delay line outputs left and right for stereo, or in the center of the stereo field for mono applications. Elaborate stereo mixing consoles will often have equalization, phase switches, _aux busses_, and other features which can help enhance the overall sound.

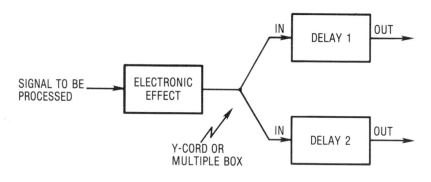

Figure 9–2

60 THROUGH-ZERO FLANGING

+ Second delay of the *same make and model* (if at all possible), mixer.

Background

Digital delay lines do not give highly dramatic flanging effects because they do not have very wide sweep ranges. In fact, most delays cannot delay less than about 0.25 to 1 ms, and cannot sweep over more than a 10:1 range (say, from 1 ms to 10 ms). Ideally, at the top end of the flanging sweep there should be *zero time difference* between the straight and delayed signals (called the *through-zero point*). In practice, though, through-zero flanging is impossible with a single delay line because it cannot delay down to 0 ms; therefore, there cannot be a zero time difference between the straight and delayed signals.

Fortunately, two delay lines can give through-zero flanging where there is an actual zero time difference between the straight and delayed signals at the top of the flange sweep. The result is a flanging sweep that seems to go infinitely high until it disappears for a tiny fraction of a second before sweeping back down again. The two delays should be of the same make and model; using dissimilar models generally gives inferior results.

The Patch

Referring to **Figure 9–3**, set both delay lines for 100 percent delayed signal and use the mixer to mix the outputs in mono. The first delay (*variable delay*) sweeps over the flanging range (for example, from 1 ms to 10 ms). The second delay (*straight delay*) is fixed at the minimum delay reached by the variable delay (in this case, 1 ms). Since the straight signal is being delayed by 1 ms, when the variable delay is at its minimum delay (1 ms), there will be zero time difference the straight and delayed signals—just what we need for through-zero flanging.

Control Settings

Set the delay line controls very carefully to experience the full effects of this patch. Both output mix controls must be set at 100 percent delayed sound, and feedback and feedback phase should be set *identically* for both delays.

Variable Delay Control Settings. Optimize the initial delay, fine delay, modulation width, and modulation speed for wide-range, fairly slow flanging (see Application 2). Initially select minimum feedback and positive feedback phase.

Fixed Delay Control Settings. If your delay has a range switch, select the same range as the variable delay. Set feedback and feedback phase the same as the variable delay, fine delay for minimum delay, and select minimum modulation width.

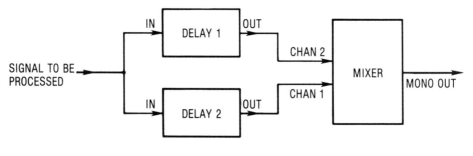

Figure 9-3

Tweaking the Patch

Listen to the peak (minimum delay point) of the flange sweep; at the magic through-zero spot, the signal will seem to disappear entirely for a fraction of a second at the very top of the flange sweep. If you're lucky, you will hear through-zero flanging immediately but chances are you will need to optimize the fixed delay's delay time. Vary the fixed delay time in small increments until the top of the flange sweep hits the through-zero point.

If the fixed delay time is longer than the minimum delay reached by the variable delay, the flange effect will sweep *beyond* the through-zero point, sweep back down a little ways, sweep up to the through-zero point again, then sweep down. If you don't like this effect, either lengthen the fixed delay time a bit, or decrease the variable delay's modulation width so that the variable delay doesn't sweep up quite so high.

For the best possible sound, carefully match the input and output levels of the two delays. Simply setting the controls identically, even with two delays of the same make and model, will not always produce identical sounds due to unit-to-unit manufacturing variations. Use your ears, not the panel markings, to judge the proper control settings.

61 CLASSIC 60s TAPE FLANGING SIMULATION

+ Second delay of the *same make and model* (if at all possible), mixer.

Background

This patch gives an even wider sweep range than Application 61, but is considerably more difficult to tweak up for the right sound.

The patch and all control settings are the same as for Application 61 except that the initial delay time settings are longer. For example, the fixed delay might be around 5 ms, with the variable delay sweeping so that its minimum delay time also hits 5 ms. The resulting flange still sweeps over a very wide range and provides the through-zero effect, but also gives a more echo-like sound towards the bottom (maximum delay) end of the flange sweep. This simulates the classic tape flanging sound that reached the peak of its popularity in the late 60s.

Longer minimum delays give even wider sweeps; however, it then becomes obvious that the straight signal is also being delayed somewhat.

62 MORE RANDOMIZED FLANGING SWEEP

+ Mixer.

Background

Sometimes the cyclic sweep of a delay line LFO can be out of sync with a song's rhythm. Although this application does not actually randomize the flanging sweep, it does make the LFO sweep less regular-sounding.

The Patch

This uses the same patch as **Figure 9–3.** Note that the mixer sums the outputs into mono.

Control Settings

The control settings are mostly the same as for standard flanging, but with some important differences.

Initial Delay. Set both delays to your favorite range for flanging effects. Set both fine delay controls to the same approximate setting. With pushbutton select delay lines, choose an initial delay time between 0 ms and 10 ms for both delays (sometimes, choosing slightly different initial delay times for the two delays gives the best sound).

Feedback (Regeneration), Feedback Phase. Choose your favorite feedback setting and set both delays identically.

Modulation Width. With slow sweeps, start off with maximum width for both delays. Trim back later if more subtlety is required.

Modulation Speed. For the most pronounced randomization effect, select a slow sweep speed and slightly offset the individual speed controls. (For example, if one modulation speed control is up 25 percent of the way, the other speed control should be just a little above or below 25 percent.)

Output Mix. Set both delays to 100 percent delayed sound, and make sure to mix the outputs in mono.

Tweaking the Patch

The crucial parameter is the offset between the two modulation speed controls; too much offset tends to create a more periodic sound, while too little offset gives a sound more like a single LFO.

63 MONO TO STEREO TO HARD STEREO CONVERSION

+ Stereo mixer.

Background

This unusual patch allows for continuously changing a mono signal from mono to stereo (with some center channel information) to hard stereo (left and right only, with very little center channel information).

The Patch

See stereo patch E. Pan one channel completely to the left, and the other channel completely to the right.

Control Settings

Initial Delay. Set one delay for about 5 or 6 ms, the other for 10 to 11 ms.
Feedback (Regeneration). Initially select minimum feedback for both delays.
Feedback Phase. Choose the same phase for both units (whether positive or negative is not important).
Modulation Width. Select minimum modulation.
Modulation Speed. It does not matter with minimum modulation.
Output Mix. For a mono output, set both controls for 100 percent straight signal. For stereo, set both controls for 50 percent straight and 50 percent delayed sounds. For hard stereo, set both controls for 100 percent delayed sound.

Tweaking the Patch

Carefully match the input and output levels of the two delays for best results. Caution: With short delays, spreading a mono source into stereo and then recombining the stereo outputs back into mono may change the tonality. (For another example of this phenomenon, see Application 6.) With long delays, you may hear an objectionable slapback echo effect. Therefore, select a delay setting that is short enough to avoid echo effects, but long enough so that the signal sounds acceptable when recombined back into mono.

64 PSYCHO-ACOUSTIC PANNING

+ Stereo mixer.

Background

This application sounds outstanding with held chords, drones, E-bow guitar, complex drum machine patterns, and the like. It is particularly effective when wearing headphones, since the sound pans and swirls inside your head. (Note that this panning is not caused by level changes, but instead by psycho-acoustic phase and delay interactions.)

The Patch

See standard stereo patch E. Pan one channel completely to the left and the other channel completely to the right.

Control Settings

Consider the following settings a point of departure; be sure to experiment.

Initial Delay. Set one delay for about 6 ms, the other for about 12 ms.

Feedback (Regeneration). Initially add about 20 percent to 50 percent feedback.

Feedback Phase. Initially select negative feedback, as it gives a somewhat gentler sound than positive feedback.

Modulation Width. Add enough modulation to be obvious, but not so much as to sound out-of-tune (about 20 percent).

Modulation Speed. The modulation speed adjusts the panning rate. Set one delay's speed control to approximately 1 Hz, then offset the other delay's speed slightly from 1 Hz.

Output Mix. Set both delays for 100 percent delayed sound.

Tweaking the Patch

When testing out this patch, wear headphones and plug a sustaining sound into the two delay inputs.

The most important controls are modulation width, modulation speed, and feedback. Increasing modulation width makes the panning more pronounced but will also make the sweep effect less even-sounding. Add as much modulation as possible, consistent with a good-sounding sweep.

The speed controls should be close to the same rate but not synchronized. If the panning effect is not apparent enough, increase the speed. Finally, feedback should be kept low enough to avoid an overly metallic tonality.

65 STEREO CHORUS THAT DOESN'T GO AWAY IN MONO

+ Stereo mixer.

Background

Most stereo choruses create a synthesized—not true—stereo chorus; playing back a synthesized stereo chorus in mono (say, over AM radio) diminishes, or, in some cases, completely removes, the chorus effect. Two delay lines can give a true stereo chorus effect that does not go away when played back in mono.

The Patch

See stereo patch E. The channels may be panned either left and right for stereo, or to center for mono.

Control Settings

The control settings are very similar to standard chorusing, except that each delay is set somewhat differently.

Initial Delay. Set one delay line for an initial delay of around 10 ms and the other for an initial delay around 20 ms.

Feedback (Regeneration). Add about 20 percent feedback to accent the chorus effect.

Feedback Phase. Initially select positive feedback.

Modulation Width. Add approximately 15 percent to 20 percent modulation to each delay (about as much as for standard mono chorusing).

Modulation Speed. Slower speeds often sound more majestic when chorusing. At faster speeds, trim modulation width somewhat. Offset the modulation speeds for the two units by a small amount.

Output Mix. For the most noticeable chorus effect, set each delay's output mix control to 50 percent straight and 50 percent delayed sound.

Tweaking the Patch

Tweak this patch similarly to standard chorusing—increase feedback for extra sharpness, change the mix to less delay for a subtler chorus effect, or shorten the delay for more of a flange/chorus sound.

66 STEREO ROOM AMBIENCE SIMULATOR

+ Stereo mixer with stereo reverb or *aux buss.*

Background

This is not the same effect as reverb, but rather produces the acoustical effect you associate with being in a small-to-moderate-sized room. The DeltaLab technical staff showed me this patch, which had been used in some very early DeltaLab products.

The Patch

Referring to **Figure 9–4**, patch the mixer's reverb *buss* outputs (sends) to the two delay line inputs. The delay line outputs feed two reverb returns (or channel inputs) at the mixer. Assuming that you have a stereo reverb *buss*, turn up the reverb send controls on the two reverb return channels. (Caution: Turn up these send controls *slowly* and *carefully*—routing some of the delayed signal back to the input, as we are doing, can cause feedback.) Now cross-pan the two reverb channel sends so that Delay 1's output is sending into the reverb channel that feeds Delay 2's input, and Delay 2's output is sending into the reverb channel that feeds Delay 1's input. A little low-frequency and high-frequency rolloff (via the mixer channel's tone controls or high-cut/low-cut switches) can tighten up the sound.

Control Settings

There are so many possibilities to this patch it's best to just settle in and play for a while. Short delays and long delays give entirely different effects, both of which can be musically effective.
Initial Delay. Initially select 25 ms for one delay and 50 ms for the other.
Feedback (Regeneration). Start off with minimum feedback, since the mixing console provides feedback externally to the delay lines. Later on, experiment with adding feedback sparingly at one or both delays.

Feedback Phase. Select positive phase.
Modulation Width. Select minimum modulation.
Modulation Speed. It does not matter with minimum modulation.
Output Mix. Since the purpose of this patch is to provide ambience behind a straight signal, set both delays for 100 percent delayed sound.

Tweaking the Patch

This patch provides many, many effects. Try different delay settings, different positions of the reverb send panpots, adding some feedback at the delay lines themselves, or changing the amount of the straight signal being sent to the reverb *buss*. While fooling around with this patch, I got everything from the ultimate garage band stereo guitar sound to highly ambient electronic drum sounds.

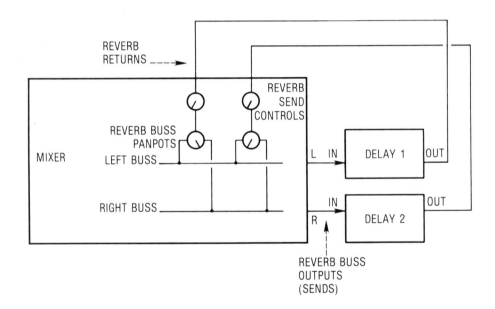

Figure 9-4

67 DOUBLE-TIME/TRIPLET STEREO EFFECTS

+ Stereo mixer, second delay line with delay time readout (ideally, both delays should have a delay time readout).

Background

This patch produces a complex drum sound with a lot of motion.

The Patch

Figure 9-5 shows one suggested patch: Straight drums panned to the center, one delay line output panned right, and the other delay line output panned left. (Note: If it's not convenient to split the drum output three ways, some delays include a *dry* or *straight* output jack that parallels the delay input. This can provide a straight drum sound for the mixer).

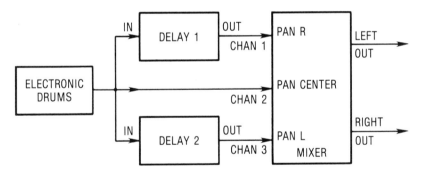

Figure 9-5

Control Settings

Both delays are basically set up for echo (see Application 13). The most critical adjustments are the delay times for each delay.

Initial Delay, Delay 1. Set the delay time equal to an eighth note (see Application 16 for information on how to set echo time to a particular rhythmic value).

Initial Delay, Delay 2. Set the delay time equal to a quarter-note triplet (again, see Application 16). Having a delay time readout on both delays is helpful; for example, if the correct delay time for delay 1 (eighth-note) is 100 ms, multiply this value by $4/3$ ($100 \times 4/3 = 133$ ms) to calculate the desired delay for delay 2.

Output Mix. Set both delay lines for 100 percent delayed output.

Tweaking the Patch

After selecting the correct delay times, vary feedback to set the number of echoes. Increasing the number of echoes gives a more diffuse, billowy sound; reducing the number of echoes gives a tighter, sharper sound.

Try panning the two delay line outputs to opposite sides of the stereo field. If this creates an overly confusing sound, pan the delay line outputs closer to center. To make the center channel sound more prominent, adjust the output mix controls for more straight sound or change the mixer settings.

Of course, double-time and triplet combinations represent only one possibility. You could also try half-time and quadruple time, two different triplet values, and so on.

68 HAAS EFFECT

+ Stereo monitoring system, mic pair, stereo mixer.

Background

The *Haas Effect* (also called the *precedence effect*) occurs by delaying *one* channel of a stereo pair; a listener hears the straight channel with greater intensity than the delayed channel (despite the fact that both channels are at equal amplitude), thus shifting the stereo image towards the straight signal. This patch, suggested by Craig O'Donnell (he calls it *Haas-in-Hell*), combines the Haas effect with acoustic space to create a controllable acoustic environment for budget studios.

The Patch

This patch (see **Figure 9-6**) requires a fairly elaborate setup and is most suited to studio applications. Treat this patch as if it was reverb; send the reverb *buss* outputs into the delay lines as shown, the delay outputs into power amps/monitors, then pick up the delayed sound and send it back into the reverb return inputs.

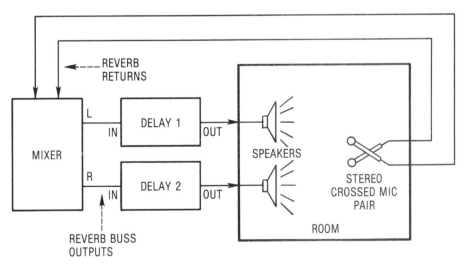

Figure 9-6

Control Settings

This is another one of those patches that has a virtually limitless number of options. All suggested settings apply to both delays used in the patch.

Initial Delay. Select a relatively short delay (less than 20 ms).

Fine Delay. Once the patch is set up, adjust to change the nature of the Haas effect.

Feedback (Regeneration). Add about 25 percent to 50 percent feedback.

Feedback Phase. Select positive feedback.

Modulation Width. Initially select about 25 percent modulation.

Modulation Speed. Select a slow-to-moderate speed.

Output Mix. Initially set the Output Mix controls for 50 percent to 100 percent delayed sound.

Tweaking the Patch

While shorter delays give the most realistic sounds, Haas lends itself to experimentation. As Craig says, "This patch is intended to show how including real acoustic space in a budget direct-to-tape studio can greatly enhance the sound of a tape". Be sure to experiment with the output mix, feedback, and feedback phase.

69 COMPOUND ECHO

Background

For our last application, here's a patch that's great for all kinds of echo experimentation. It gives compound echo effects, meaning that two echoes occur simultaneously and interact with each other.

The Patch

See standard patch C; patch the second delay into the first delay's feedback loop jacks.

Control Settings

Experiment!
Initial Delay. Changing the time difference between the two delay lines yields different effects. Initially set one delay to about 150 ms and the other between 175 ms and 200 ms.
Feedback (Regeneration). Adjust feedback on each delay for the desired number of echoes.
Feedback Phase. Select positive feedback.
Modulation Width. Initially select minimum modulation.
Modulation Speed. It does not matter with minimum modulation.
Output Mix. Initially set the output mix controls for both units at 50 percent straight and 50 percent delayed sound.

Tweaking the Patch

The crucial controls are feedback and output mix. This patch can create numerous echo effects; experiment and enjoy.